STEPHEN THE CHINESE PASTOR

Also by Mary Wang

THE CHINESE CHURCH THAT WILL NOT DIE

STEPHEN THE CHINESE PASTOR

The life of Stephen Wang is part of the
heroic story of the Chinese Church

by

MARY WANG

with Gwen and Edward England

HODDER AND STOUGHTON
LONDON   SYDNEY   AUCKLAND   TORONTO

To the spiritual children
of Stephen Wang

Acknowledgments

I am indebted to all those who contributed memories and documents about Stephen Wang, including members of the Chinese Churches in London, Manchester and on the Continent. In particular I would like to mention Dr. and Mrs. F. Pyke in America; a former pupil of Stephen Wang now resident in Norway; the Rev. Fred Harding, C.O.C.M. Treasurer; Dr. A. J. Broomhall, Mr. David Adeney, Miss Phyllis Thompson, Sister Gladys Stephenson, Mr. Chua Wee Hian, Mr. Frank Cheung, Mr. Alfred Bosshardt; the librarian of the Methodist Missionary Society, and the editor of *The Methodist Recorder*.

Most of all I would like to thank my friends Gwen and Edward England who put the words on paper for me.

MARY WANG

Foreword

by David H. Adeney

MANY BOOKS and articles are being written these days by visitors to the mainland of China. Often they can only give a superficial view of certain sections of the society which have been carefully prepared as a show piece for the West.

This book is completely different. It does not claim to give a picture of present day China. But it does provide valuable insights into the history of both the pre-war Church and the Church that remained under the Communist regime.

Mary Wang, the author, passed through great spiritual conflicts in 1955, when as a medical student in Shanghai she was detained during the summer vacation for political studies. She can write, therefore, with deep understanding not only of Stephen Wang before and after he left China, but also of his family who remained within the Communist society.

Whenever Christians are called to pass through experiences of suffering and persecution God raises up men of faith whose lives shine as beacons in the darkness witnessing to the reality of the living Christ.

Some like Wang Ming-Tao and Watchman Nee and great numbers whose names are not known, have faithfully followed their Lord in prisons and labour camps of China. Among these was Sung Ling, Stephen Wang's own daughter, whose faith was an inspiration to the author in her student days. Others, like Stephen Wang himself, are delivered from prison and given the freedom to live a long life of service.

Stephen's life bridged the gap between the old China, with its freedom of Christian witness and the new China in which Communism claims complete control over the minds of the people.

Stephen also formed a link between the hidden suffering Church in China and Chinese Christians of the dispersion. With his wife and children in China Stephen Wang was a constant reminder of the importance of praying for the Church of the Lord Jesus on the mainland. His own prayer life was divided between those whom he loved in his homeland, and the new members of the Household of God who were being gathered out from among the Chinese scattered throughout the western countries.

For those of us who have lived in China Stephen Wang's story brings back many memories. We arrived in China five years after he commenced his work as headmaster of Tangshan Methodist School. Our ministry on the mainland of China ended two years after Stephen left for England. We also lived under the Communist regime working among the university students in Shanghai, and Mary Wang, who was then a student, read the accusations against us which were published in the wall newspapers after we left China.

The story of Stephen's early life throws light on the growth of the Church before the revolution. We see especially the way in which God was calling out Chinese leadership for the Church. Trials and suffering during the war with Japan helped to purify many of those who were to be the spiritual leaders under Communist rule. Stephen's candid discussions with missionary leaders reveal both the strengths and weaknesses of the missionary movement. It does not gloss over misunderstandings that sometimes arose between missionaries and their Chinese fellow workers, but it shows also the deep love that bound together men and women from the East and from the West in the fellowship of the Gospel.

Although we cannot remember actually meeting in China we may well have worshipped together in the church of which Wang Ming-Tao was the pastor. Stephen was deeply influenced by the courageous testimony of this man of God who under both Japanese and Communist regimes resolutely proclaimed Christ, refusing to allow his church to be used by any political movement. I was in their church for the first student prayer conference in 1946 when Christian Fellowships were being started in the universities of Peking, and well remember his powerful messages during the Evangelistic campaign which followed. We bade farewell to Wang Ming-Tao in 1950, and together with great numbers of Chinese Christians as well as Western fellow workers remember him with deep affection. This book will remind the reader to pray for Wang Ming-Tao and many others who are in labour camps "on account of the Word of God and the testimony of Jesus."

Later Stephen's daughter Sung Ling was greatly helped by Pastor David Yang, a man whose friendship had meant a tremendous amount to me, dating back to an experience in the early thirties when I was a member of his 'Spiritual Work Team' in Shansi.

Thus when I met Stephen in London at the Chinese Church we had much in common. I remember him at a church conference referring to his little notebook with the names of those who had recently come to Christ. I know from my own personal experience that he was a man with a real pastor's heart, for I was much impressed by his gracious concern when he visited me as a patient in the Mildmay Hospital.

Since then in Hong Kong and Singapore I have met numbers of Chinese students whose spiritual home was the Chinese Church in London. The effect of his ministry is still seen in many a home and church in Southeast Asia.

This book will be read not only by hundreds who have known Stephen Wang as a true shepherd in the Church, but also by great numbers who are concerned for the fulfillment of God's purpose for Chinese Christians throughout the world. They will indeed agree with Stephen Wang's words, "If China is to be evangelised it must be by the Chinese. A foreign shaped Christianity is not for China." They will also rejoice that the author of this book, who has given us such an inspiring account of his life, is now continuing his work. Having lived under Communism in China before pioneering work among Chinese nurses in England, Mary Wang, who for so long served as a daughter to the beloved pastor, is indeed qualified to lead the Chinese Overseas Christian Mission. Her book will surely be used to present to the readers, and especially to Chinese young people the vision that motivated Stephen Wang. Out from this generation of young Chinese there must come dedicated servants of the living Christ, for the Chinese Church 'will never die'.

David H. Adeney
Discipleship Training Centre,
Singapore.

Contents

Prologue

THE LIFE of Stephen Wang is the story of a Chinese Christian gentleman. It is also part of the heroic story of the Chinese Church.

His biography is a reminder of those revolutionary events from the Boxer Rebellion in 1900 to the Red Guards closing the last of the Christian churches in 1966. If he barely spoke of these things it was because he chose to talk of his living faith, to open the pages of his worn Chinese Bible pointing to a treasured passage, but he had observed the savage suffering and shared its heartbreak.

A missionary was once asked, "What sort of Christians do the Chinese make?"

"All sorts, just as at home," he replied.

In the story of the Chinese Church there are tares among the wheat, there are Christians who denied their faith in days of persecution, and became persecutors themselves, but for a century there have been believers who have died for Christ, refusing to recant, even when they could have saved their lives by doing so.

The torment of Christians did not start with the proclamation of the Communist People's Republic of China. As long as Stephen could remember in some area or other Christians were liable to be kidnapped, murdered and held to ransom. Christian villages in places like Shantung were razed to the ground. Church services were violently interrupted, with Bibles, hymnbooks and personal belongings being burned, schools disbanded, buildings destroyed. Chinese pastors were insulted, beaten, or terrorised.

"But," wrote one missionary, "they survived the test in a truly remarkable way, counting it an honour to suffer for the sake of the Name. I well remember an elder of our Church saying in all sincerity that he hoped Christ would deem him worthy to be beaten or stoned."

Stephen was proud to be associated by name with the first Christian martyr. It was an honourable name for one who was the product of a Church which had experienced bandits, imprisonments, torture, brain-washing and labour camps, a Church which was cradled in suffering.

He was born in north China in 1900 when more than sixteen thousand Chinese Christians and over two hundred missionaries were killed in the uprising which swept through north and north-west China. The Boxers, originally incensed by drought and flood in Shantung, turned against the missionaries, their religion and its adherents.

As a boy he knew the face of poverty.

When he was eight a Chinese Christian pastor and his family came to his village; knowing his parents would not reprimand him he gleefully stoned the pastor's sons, then became the first Christian convert in the village.

The outbreak of the Chinese Revolution took place when he was eleven, and the next year the Manchu dynasty abdicated, setting up by imperial decree a republic as its successor. He was twenty-one when the Chinese Communist Party was founded at a secret meeting in the French Concession of Shanghai. Among the twelve delegates from various parts of the country was Mao Tse-tung, who had started the Hunan cell. There were about fifty members of the Party at this time, but when the Party's third meeting took place in 1923 the membership was 432. It had organised in Shanghai and the south more than one hundred strikes.

Stephen witnessed the onslaught of the Anti-Christian Movement. At twenty-nine he became headmaster of the

Tangshan Methodist school in Hopei, north China, remaining in this position during the Japanese occupation.

In 1948 he travelled to England to study in Cambridge.

On January 21, 1949, Chiang Kai-shek resigned the Presidency of the Republic of China and the Government moved to Taiwan. On October 1 the Communist People's Republic of China was officially proclaimed at Peking with Mao Tse-tung as Chairman, and Chou En-lai as Premier. Because of the Communist takeover it was dangerous for Stephen to return to China, so as an exile from his own country he commenced his most effective ministry, founding the Chinese Church in London, and the Chinese Overseas Christian Mission, with branches around the world, including America. But in the West he was always thinking and praying for the Church in China.

Until 1964 he received letters from his daughter, who in 1958 had been sent to a labour camp for her faith. His wife, and other children, were still in China, a China whose face had been completely changed.

"By the year 2001 China will have undergone even greater changes," declared Chairman Mao. "She will have become a powerful, socialist, industrial country."

When the Chinese Red Armies gained possession of the whole of China in 1949 the shape of the world changed, but the world absorbed by its domestic policies did not recognise the consequences.

The thrust of Christian mission altered.

China had always been a dramatic, colourful mission-field. It had been the home of many of the finest missionaries, men and women of intellectual capacity, and spiritual discernment, whose courage rivalled that of the early Church. Men like Hudson Taylor, founder of the China Inland Mission, who went out in 1865 'under a deep sense of China's pressing need'. A century later that need remained but under China's new management there was no place for missionaries.

A Chinese Christian wrote: "It is clear that Communism is a religionless system and its attitude to Christianity and the Christian Church is unfavourable." In 1950 the C.I.M. sent a message to the home countries: "Pray, possibly facing the darkest period in Mission's history, but what saith the answer of God."

The Communist victory had thrown the life of Stephen Wang into a new orbit. When he said goodbye to his wife in Peking to visit Britain he did not know he would never return. The decisive battle of Huai Hai had not been fought, a battle which meant the Nationalist Party had lost the war. When he held his daughter Sung Ling he would not have released her if he had known she would live in a labour camp. But no one knew, no one guessed, statesman or Church leader, what would happen. In world terms it was a news-story which just rated the front page, yet China's second Long March had begun.

The Church was ill-prepared.

Stephen owed a substantial debt to the missionaries, but Chairman Mao and his subordinates called them a menace. Stephen had become a Christian through their example and their words; he obtained his education through their schools, but Chairman Mao listed their misdeeds. They had intruded into China's interior. He alleged they had plotted imperialist aggression, and had been a party to unequal treaties. He asserted they had meddled in China's internal affairs and acted as spies. Religion in China, the Party declared, must 'absolutely be separated from the foreign aggressionist and counter-revolutionary activities'.

However false the accusations, to be associated with missions was to be under suspicion and his association had been close. Not only had he been taught by missionaries, but he had been a headmaster in their school. Not only had he eaten at their table, but they had eaten, and often, at his. Not only had he accepted their God, but he had been given a Biblical name. He had financially supported their work and he was on their payroll.

When Stephen was advised not to return to Peking, he planned for his family to join him in England. In the West they would be free to live, think and speak as they wished, and the opportunities were plentiful for children. It was a dream, unfulfilled. In 1949 his wife could have left, but she could not be parted from her children, then the door closed, with him out and her in. In the twenty years of concentrated work which followed he was not to have the support and love of the one to whom he had turned in major decisions. Few had previously depended more upon a partner. Some letters came from her but for six years before he died there was no word, and he assumed she had died.

No man was more aware of the peril of those who followed Christ in Red China, and his concern reached beyond his own family. When he heard of 'reactionaries in religious clothing' being imprisoned for dishonesty, for endangering the lives of the masses, raping women and girls, and disturbing the peace, he was not deceived. He knew the methods of the revolutionaries. When his friend the American Ambassador to China, Dr. J. Leighton Stuart, was described as a spy he was too sad to laugh. Likewise when he heard of a preacher who was said to have caused the death, either directly or indirectly, of more than twenty people; and of a preacher who baptised seventy converts and by so doing seriously obstructed construction work.

Yet, while grieving over the brutalities and loss of liberty suffered by his fellow countrymen, he did not subscribe to the view that Red China was to be vilified on every count.

"What is the most precious thing on earth?" Mao asked. "It is man ... our people are poor and blank but the most beautiful poem can be written on a blank sheet of paper."

Stephen agreed but he wanted Christ to be the poet. And He did not need a blank sheet.

In his exile God gave him a primary vision, a passion for reaching the Chinese in the West. It was a vision from which he initially turned; it was too uncomfortable, too exacting, but he was never to escape it.

In 1950, after his months in Cambridge and lecturing at the Selly Oak Colleges, he responded by founding the Chinese Church in London. The miracle was not the starting of the Church, but that he should start it; God had been remoulding the ambitious educationalist who came to London. With one distinguished career behind him, at fifty he found the finger of God no longer pointing to the top of the career ladder. Once in China he had made an issue of securing a big salary, now he asked for none.

Once he directed school life in well-proportioned buildings, but now he was content to meet with a small group in a tiny flat.

In over-crowded Hong Kong it would have been easy for us not to meet. Wang was a common name and we were not related. It was 1961 and he had journeyed from England to negotiate, if possible, for the release of his wife from Communist China. She had been in prison but was now back in Peking and he had sought the help of the British Government in getting her to the West. But God did not allow.

"Have I, Lord, mistaken your guidance in making this trip across the world? Should I have stayed in London?" The prayer was in secret. He had been so sure that he had been prompted by God to make this further effort. "Lord, you must have some purpose."

He concealed his brokenness, his intense helplessness, but there were many in Hong Kong who shared the same agonies and kept the same sensible silence. For a shorter time my own family had experienced the frustrations of separation.

I was a student in mainland China until 1957. Most of my family had previously reached Hong Kong, my preacher-father in January 1951 because of Communist persecution. Those were days when many were being imprisoned, or shot as counter-revolutionaries. Father had removed a portrait of Chairman Mao from his church because it desecrated the House of God, and he had to escape one night when charges were brought against him.

In those months it was not unusual in various parts of China to see early morning processions on their way to execution, sometimes six or twelve, sometimes eighty or more.

My brother, Michael, helped father to reach Hong Kong, while my mother was left to support the remaining children, Martin, Ruby and myself. It was eight years before we all reached Hong Kong, but as a family how fortunate we were when others who had not responded to persuasion, re-education and thought reform, had been sentenced after summary trials at mass meetings. We had left friends in labour camps for being 'enemies of the people'.

I was a student at the Christian and Missionary Alliance seminary taking a Bachelor of Theology course. Stephen addressed the morning chapel in the seminary, preaching from Jeremiah 18 on the marred vessel that might have been discarded but was remade by the potter. It was how he saw himself. I was the pianist that morning, but did not know that years before Stephen had been a college student with my father. Later, my father introduced me, and he told us of the need for a girl like myself to assist in ministering to the hundreds of Chinese nurses in England.

Although he said little of his disappointment at not being able to secure the freedom of his wife, or daughter Sung Ling, he revealed how his daughter had been sentenced to ten years and sent to north-west China. Now she had tuberculosis of the spine.

Nine months later, in September 1961, I arrived in London to begin my nurse's training at the King Edward Memorial Hospital, Ealing, situated within easy reach of the Chinese Church. Pastor Wang lived in the House of Rest, used by missionaries and Christian workers, and on days off with other students and nurses I visited him there.

King Ling cared for his material needs. She had been converted in London, later secured her Ph.D. at London University, and in 1962, married Chua Wee-hian, the assistant pastor.

King Ling, in her early twenties, became the honorary secretary of the Chinese Church, and I admired and envied her. She had compassion and confidence, in a gentle, quiet way. When pastor mentioned how he missed his family she reminded him of the sons and daughters, and they were numerous, which he now had in the Chinese Church. One morning he asked her to come to his room directly after breakfast. He waited impatiently until ten o'clock.

"Wherever have you been?" he demanded.

"Pastor," she replied, gently, "I had someone more important to meet first," referring to her morning devotion.

I was so startled by what she achieved, with calmness and dignity, that slightly embarrassed I offered to assist. I had weekends off during the first part of training as a nurse and so did the laundry for Stephen, while she prepared her thesis. Unexpectedly, I found myself at the heart of things, preparing a meal for visitors, coping with washing, scribbling letters, making phone calls.

"Pastor," someone said, "you always find girls to help you."

"I like girls around me," he laughed, "because when the girls are there the boys come too."

There were many weddings and he liked conducting these, but was tense before one because he had once talked of the Bread and Breadgroom.

My English was shaky, but I wrote letters for him in Chinese, many at times, and because I called him uncle other residents in the House of Rest thought I was a niece.

Letters to my family in Hong Kong were occupied with him: he did, he said, we went. There was little mention of London, although the throb of the metropolis was on the doorstep.

"I will write to your parents and ask them to give you to me so that you can be my daughter," he said, when I had not done as he wished. "Then I can shout and correct you and you will have to listen."

I quoted him in my next letter. It would have been easy for my parents to be jealous. For several years while in China I had been cut off from them, but they wrote how wonderful it would be if I were his daughter, filling a bit of the gap. He missed his family terribly, yet to most he rarely spoke of the well-bred, beautiful woman he had married, and of his three sons and two daughters.

My family came from the same province in north China as his wife, and all from there were dear to him. He listened for the accent, the turn of phrase.

In July 1962 he took a holiday at the gracious home of Mrs. Marjorie Hurnard in Colchester. He went for two weeks most summers, taking correspondence with him. I arranged to spend four days there; I could write letters, and give him news from the Church. On the evening before I returned to London we sat together in the garden. There was a slight breeze at the close of a pleasant day. In the peace of that garden, surrounded by summer flowers, he opened his heart.

"Mary," he asked, "are you willing to uphold me in my work?"
I did not have to reply, hurt that he should ask.

"Mary, do you care enough to be with me whatever tomorrow holds?"

I looked at this man, revealing his soul, with one goal, to show the Chinese his God. Because he gave himself, he expected likewise. He was too demanding, unconscious of mealtimes, that it was late in the day, or that leisure was part of God's timetable. He was old, unmusical, but to a degree I had rarely seen he served Christ. I was challenged that he should consider sharing the vision God had entrusted with such an immature person.

God has a habit of saying no, then showing us another route. In China I wanted to study music. With four hundred pupils I took the entrance examinations in Shanghai, but because of my Christian testimony I was not accepted.

I spent four years training to be a doctor. It meant even more to me than music. I passed my examinations but to be registered as a doctor I had to complete a fifth year. But God's plan was that instead I should go to Hong Kong and so I was never registered. My four years medical training was not recognised outside the mainland. My disappointment was so intense that I went through an emotional crisis, in which I was a great trial to my family.

I graduated after three years in a Bible seminary and looked forward to full-time Christian service in Hong Kong but God had another plan. I was given an air ticket to London for training as a nurse.

Now I was faced with a fresh vision.

"Uncle," I said, "I will not only be with you whatever the future, but so that I can do this fully I make a second promise." It was dusk and the lights were being switched on in the house where we had been made so welcome. "Uncle, while you need me I will not marry."

"You must not say things like that," he replied, lifting his eyes. And then was lost for words. "Think it over," he later said.

"I don't need to," I whispered. "Uncle, I know."

He cried a little. We started back towards the house passing the flowers which made a splash of colour in the reflected light. The other guests retired for the night and the house settled down, but for a while I did not sleep.

I had always sensed there was a reason why God had allowed my escape from Communist China. Now I knew.

Later, he told me how when he was in Hong Kong and learned that his wife could not leave China, and that Sung Ling was not to be released, that he asked God for an assurance that he would be able to survive in the face of this separation.

"Do you remember, Mary, how I met you before I left Hong Kong? Your father brought you to my hotel and then he hurried away to attend an appointment. I sat you down and I looked at you, the daughter of my old college friend. Do you remember?"

I shook my head.

"When I saw you I knew that your presence in London would be to me God's assurance of future strength."

I was to have nine years by his side. There were days when I regretted the promise I had made, no hours, then I remembered how God in his mercy had brought me into the free world. I thought of Sung Ling, his lovely daughter with such high hopes, who was still in China.

"Our Heavenly Father, we praise thee, we thank you . . ." Invariably, he started his prayer this way. As I think of him, the same words come to my lips. His capacity for love was a rebuke. He carried us to a higher level. Let go of earthly things and aim for the highest, he urged. If you will, you can do almost anything.

This is his story . . .

PART ONE

I

The Boy

THE LITTLE BOY Yu-teh (he was not Stephen yet), was unusually bright but there was little hope of him being anything but his father's image, a farmer and a profiteer, worshipping the family's ancestral tablets and the Buddhist idol in the hill-top shrine.

Yu-teh was born in a tiny village, adjacent to the twin tracks of the Chinese Eastern Railway in north China, a stone's throw from the mini-station known as An Shan, a low hill crowned by a bare little temple that looked as though no one ever climbed the steep ascent to burn joss sticks before the impassive idol.

The railway was the link with the mysterious world outside, but only the 'little fast train' ever deigned to stop there. The 'big fast train' and the Trans-Siberian Special that ended in Paris, always went by in a swirl of dust and noise, leaving the primitive countryside to pursue its placid ways, scarcely changed in a thousand years. Most of the villagers had never been more than a few miles beyond its borders.

"A man does not travel to distant places when his parents are living," Confucius said, "and if he does he must have a definite destination."

As a boy Yu-teh liked to listen to the story-teller who travelled from street to street and from village to village. One day he was greatly pleased to learn the story about the first man of China.

His name was Pan Ku. The heaven and earth were in chaos. When Pan Ku was born, he grew ten feet higher each day, and the heaven rose up ten feet apart from the earth and the earth became ten feet thicker. After 18,000 years Pan Ku died. His bones became the five great mountains, his eyes became the sun and moon, and his blood became rivers and streams. The story suggested a mathematical problem which appealed to his mind. If he knew the total number of days in 18,000 years he could calculate the height of heaven and the thickness of the earth. Later, when he was told it was not a true story, he was very disappointed.

Yu-teh's neighbours were largely poor, peaceful hard-working peasants, but something happened of which they strongly disapproved. He could hear them grumbling and growling about the matter. The foreign religion 'Jesus Way' was opening a Gospel hall on the main street, and they wanted nothing to do with it. It was an intrusion they would oppose.

It was shortly after the Anti-Foreign Agitation, popularly known as the Boxer uprising, which had as its motto: "To protect the country and to destroy the foreigners." The Boxers were angry at the seizure of territory by foreign powers, resentful against the alleged interference of missionaries in lawsuits, and Chinese institutions and customs.

The elders in the small village by the railway gathered to discuss the opening of the Gospel Hall. His parents spoke in the most unkind and disparaging manner, wanting to 'run it out of town'. It was Yu-teh's introduction to the foreign religion.

It always took courage to be a pastor or missionary.

The first Christian missionaries in China were probably the Nestorians in the seventh century. They came from the Eastern Church in central Asia and were named Nestorians after their leader Nestorius. They established themselves in almost every province over a period of two hundred years, then came severe persecution and for four centuries the Christian voice was silenced.

In 1294 the Pope sent John of Montecorvino to the Emperor, and he gained favour of the court. He bought 150 poor boys of pagan parents to teach them Latin and Greek. After ten years he baptised 6,000 converts, and in 1307 was made Archbishop of Peking. He died in 1328 and the Emperor of Cathay requested the Pope to send a new Archbishop, which he did, but there were constant set-backs, partly because 'they tried to foreignise the Chinese, or at least they remained obstinately foreign themselves'.

There was a lack of native ministry, always foreign leadership, and imperial protection and patronage produced a backlash. The church was criticised for having started at the top of society.

Robert Morrison was the first Protestant missionary to China, and he reached Canton on September 7, 1807 as the representative of the London Missionary Society. His first ambition had been to go to Africa, but in college he responded to the call to China, and in London learned Chinese with a Chinese student. He sailed to China via America because the East India Company was hostile to missionary work.

He was twenty-five when he arrived.

He found that not only the Chinese government were hostile but that the Roman Catholic priests were hostile, but because of his knowledge of Chinese in 1808 he was given a post as interpreter to the East India Company. He gave six or eight hours of each day to translating the Bible and to composing a Chinese dictionary. During his first twenty-five years in China there were ten baptisms.

When Morrison died after twenty-seven years there were only two other Protestant missionaries in China, both of whom belonged to the American Board of Missions.

Several new missions arrived in China in the next twenty-five years, including the Church Missionary Society, the American Southern Baptists, the American Protestant Episcopal Church, English and American Presbyterians, and the American Southern Methodist Mission.

The first Protestant missionary hospital in the world developed out of the medical work started by Dr. Peter Parker in Canton, in 1835. At first there were no nurses, no Chinese textbooks, no schools of nursing, not even a word in the language for nurse. The hospital was an old mud house, the operating room a corner of the verandah boarded up and mudded over. The patients came in, bringing their own food, and relatives to care for them. They wore their own clothes and objected to baths.

Methodism, which was to have such an influence in Yu-teh's life, opened in China in 1852 when George Piercy entered into its service in Canton.

In 1864 the first Methodist medical missionary was employed in Central China, but his success made the appointment of a woman doctor imperative as with 'the commonest and severest female maladies Chinese sentiment forbids a man to interpose'. The lady doctor sent to Hankow was Louisa Sugden, a woman of exceptional ability and courage, who accomplished great things. She soon required a hospital, but there was no money. One day she was visiting a poor invalid who said, "You are going to have your hospital. God has told me so. And look! here is a bit of gold to start it with!"

The Hankow Women's Hospital was opened in 1888. Geographically, it was a fine situation for 'there was no other important city in the world so far inland, which could be reached by ocean liners'.

It might be imagined that the arrival of missionaries, whether as doctors, teachers, or evangelists would have been welcomed, but in writing of missionary enterprise in China it is impossible not to refer to the country's history, and at this point to the opium trade.

Opium was probably introduced to China by the Arabs. The Portuguese and the Dutch traded in the drug, but later the trade passed into the hands of the British. The five-volume history *The Wesleyan Methodist Missionary Society*, by Findlay and Holdsworth, claims that the attitude of the British East India Company to this trade was most reprehensible.

This chapter of English history is not one which any right-minded Englishman can contemplate without shame, and if from that time the foreigner was exposed to the execrations of the Chinese it is not a matter at which anyone can be surprised ... The traders had filled their coffers, but they had smirched the fair name of England ... Into this evil inheritance the missionary entered by the mere fact that he belonged to the hated race ... For years to come the missionaries were forced to accept the sorry protection of the British gun-boat in the treaty-port.

In the nineteenth century, before the Boxer uprising, Chinese Christians faced persecution. Placards were carried inciting violence. One placard, not untypical, read:

One who has been bewitched by the spies of foreign devils, and has the religion of Jesus, is to be dragged immediately to the ancestral temple and severely dealt with by the clan. He must be compelled to forsake his depraved heresy and return to the right way. Should he refuse to obey, the clan shall take the entire family of the pig-goat-devil, old and young, male and female, and drive them out of the place.

In Hunan those who met a missionary were instructed to 'act as maybe most expedient, rob him of his money, strip him of his clothes, deprive him of his food, or cut off his ears and nose'.

On June 5, 1891 a Chinese man was seen carrying four children to receive the blessing of a Roman Catholic priest. When the man was asked if he was taking the children to be killed he jokingly answered, "Yes". A riot started and in the crush one of the children was killed. Mission houses were burned. William Argent, a Methodist missionary, and a member of the Customs Service were killed in brutal fashion. Four new Methodist missionaries were at once appointed to take Mr. Argent's place.

The Roman Catholic Church's allegiance to a foreign Pope was misunderstood. The Church of the Heavenly Lord found that the wits changed one Chinese character so that it became the Church of the Land Lord. The Chinese had been forced to accept that Roman Catholic bishops were of rank equal to a viceroy, while priests received a magistrate's status. It irked. The Protestants refused to accept the rank. Priests and nuns were suspected of hiding strange things under their unusual garments.

The China Inland Mission sent its first missionaries in 1865.

In 1897 two Roman Catholic Priests were killed in Shantung. They were of German nationality and the German government availed itself of this opportunity of intervention. There was much bargaining among other foreign powers, and the dividing of the nation seemed imminent. The Chinese sought to save the situation by bringing into existence the Reform Movements.

The Reformers believed that hatred of the foreigners was neither justifiable nor healthy, and that mutual friendships could be cultivated with advantage. They recognised that the ancient system was inadequate and struggled to adopt Western learning. Some even went so far as to advocate the adoption of Christianity as the national religion in place of Confucianism. By the close of 1899 the Emperor was imprisoned in Ying-tai and the Reform Movements had come to an end.

The Anti-Foreign Agitation started a general persecution of Christians in parts of north China.

Among the Roman Catholics five bishops and forty-two priests and sisters were killed. Among Chinese Catholics some say that more than thirty thousand were killed or died from privation. Between two hundred and four hundred out of seven hundred Russian Orthodox communicants were killed.

Among the Protestants 186 missionaries and children died, and slightly more than a third of these were members of the China Inland Mission. It is calculated that almost two thousand Protestant Chinese Christians died, but most of those who survived remained true to their faith.

A Boxer edict 'issued by the Lord of Wealth and Happiness' gives a clue to the peril which faced all Christians. It said:

The Catholic and Protestant religions being insolent to the gods, and extinguishing sanctity, rendering no obedience to Buddha, and enraging Heaven and Earth, the rain clouds no longer visit us; but eight million Spirit Soldiers will descend from Heaven and sweep the Empire clean of all foreigners. Then will the gentle showers once more water our lands; and when the tread of soldiers and the clash of steel are heard heralding woes to all our people, then the Buddhist Patriotic

League of Boxers will be able to protect the Empire and to bring peace to all its people.

Hasten, then, to spread this doctrine far and wide, for if you gain one adherent to the faith, your own person will be absolved from all future misfortunes. If you gain five adherents your whole family will be absolved from all evils, and if you gain ten adherents your whole village will be absolved from all calamities. Those who gain no adherents to the cause shall be decapitated, for until all foreigners have been exterminated the rain can never visit us.

The first martyr of the uprising was an Englishman, Mr. Brooks, aged twenty-four, who had arrived with the S.P.G. mission in Shantung two years earlier. In 1894 he had entered St. Augustine's college. Several months before his death he had a remarkable dream that he was again at St. Augustine's college, that he had read once more the names on the cloister walls, and also in the Memorial Chapel. "Then he noticed on one of the walls a space reserved exclusively for the names of martyrs who had belonged to the college. As he gazed at the space he noticed no name thereon, until gradually as he looked some letters stood out upon the wall, and he read the characters which spelled his own name."

From that day he believed he would die a violent death.

After spending Christmas with his sister who had recently arrived in China, on Friday December 29, 1899, he set out on a donkey, passing a night on the road. The following day near his destination he was set upon, pulled off his donkey, and taken outside the village of Chang-chia-tien. He escaped from his captors and being an athlete soon outdistanced his pursuers; but men on horseback overtook him, cut him down with their swords and decapitated him, throwing his body into a ravine by the roadside.

There were approximately 350 million Chinese at the turn of the century, but of these only a tiny minority had ever seen a foreigner, but they were emotionally involved in the uprising.

On August 3, 1900, Mrs. Atwater, of the American Board of Fenchow wrote:

My dear, dear ones. I have tried to gather courage to write to you once more. How am I to write all the horrible details of these days? I would rather spare you. The dear ones at Shouyang, seven in all, including our lovely girls, were taken prisoner and brought to Taiyuan in irons, and there by the Governor's orders beheaded, together with the Taiyuan friends, thirty-three souls. The following days the Roman Catholic priests and nuns from Taiyuan were also beheaded, ten souls yesterday. Three weeks after these had perished, our Mission at Taku was attacked, and our six friends there, and several brave Christians who stood by them, were beheaded. We are now waiting our call home . . .

Dear ones, I long for a sight of your dear faces, but I fear we shall not meet on earth. I have loved you all so much, and know you will not forget the one who lies in China. There never were sisters and brothers like mine. I am preparing for the end very quietly and calmly. The Lord is wonderfully near and he will not fail me. I was very restless and excited while there seemed a chance of life, but God has taken away that feeling, and now I just pray for grace to meet the terrible end bravely. The pain will soon be over, and oh the sweetness of the welcome above.

My little baby will go with me. I think God will give it to me in Heaven, and my dear mother will be so glad to see us. I cannot imagine the Saviour's welcome. Oh, that will compensate for all these days of suspense . . . I do not regret coming to China, but I am sorry I have done so little. My married life, two precious years has been so full of happiness. We will die together, my dear husband and I. I used to dread separation. If we escape now it will be a miracle. I send my love to you all, and the dear friends who remember me. Your loving sister.

In Taiyuan, on July 9, 1900, forty-five foreigners were beheaded, thirty-three Protestants and twelve Roman Catholics. A number of Chinese Christians were also killed. Their bodies were left where they fell until next morning when some of their heads were placed in cages on the city wall.

In Shansi the China Inland Mission had eighty-eight workers in 1900; forty-seven of these were killed.

In his classic *A Thousand Miles of Miracle in China*, published in 1904, and still in print, Archibald E. Glover, said:

Speaking generally, hatred of the foreigner is in the blood of the Chinaman. This natural hatred has from generation to generation been fostered by a national exclusiveness born of an overwhelming pride which boasts that the world is square, China a circle within it touching the four sides, and the four corners outside the circle the domain of the foreign barbarians. And of late years it has been fed by an even deepening suspicion of the design of foreign nations founded upon one demand for territory after another.

Missionaries hid in the mountains, sleeping in caves, often drenched by heavy rain, unwashed, unshaved, resting their feet in a creek of water, with their clothes in rags after being caught in the dense scrub.

"We were without food, but two thieves brought us bread," wrote one. "About midnight we were aroused by cries of 'Kill, kill, kill'. We remained in those caves six weeks. We used to sit up at night and watch for the wolves; during those lonely hours I felt the presence of the Lord preciously real."

In the town of Sin-pin-pu there was a congregation of three hundred members, a large proportion being merchants and farmers. Their goods and property were taken and every man, woman and child belonging to the Church who was arrested was mercilessly and often barbarously put to death.

In Peking a schoolgirl belonging to the Methodist mission was faced with fifty armed soldiers. Not far away were the corpses of about seven Christians who had been hacked to pieces. "O Lord Jesus," she prayed, "give me courage to witness for thee until the end."

Are you a Christian?" she was asked.

"I am."

"Of what church?"

"I am a Protestant."

A stick of incense was placed in her hand and she was told: "Burn this to the gods and your life will be saved."

"Never," she replied.

"Kill her, kill her, and see if her body will rise again and go to Jesus," the jeering crowd shouted.

"My body cut in pieces," she replied, "will remain scattered on the ground as these others, but my spirit will escape you and rise to God."

A chapel-keeper was bound to a pillar. He kept preaching to the persecutors. One of the Boxers angrily cried, "You still preach do you?" and slit his mouth from ear to ear. A Bible woman was bound to the same pillar and beaten across the breasts, but remained completely silent. Lighted incense was held to her face till no flesh remained, then her hands and feet were cut off. Finally, she was burned.

The Boxers spread absurd stories about the Christians.

It was alleged that Christians hired beggars to poison the village wells, and to make a mark with some red substance on the doors of houses, the inhabitants of which would become very ill or die. Great terror was spread by these reports, and in the panic many were killed who had no connection with Christianity.

When a sixty-year-old man refused to say where the missionaries were hiding he was beaten with bamboo canes and then, when nearly insensible, was thrown into prison, his feet being put in wooden stocks. On the fourth day in prison he died.

Some had the soles of their feet burned with hot irons, others were burned to death in chapels or homes which had been set alight. Mothers with their children were driven into the flames at the point of a sword.

"This is the happiest day of my life," said one shortly before he was killed with the sword.

"Leave the foreign sect and you will not be killed," the believers were told.

Some who did leave the Church to find protection returned to their homes to find that nevertheless they had been pillaged and burned.

In a mission in Shantung several Chinese pastors recanted to save their people.

"Is it not right to do wrong for such a cause?" they asked.

Later, they repented and handed in their resignations, but they were prevailed upon to withdraw them because of the weak state of the Church. The missionary present wrote how in broken accents and voices trembling with emotion, each of the pastors humbly confessed the sin of which he had been guilty, and asked the forgiveness of the Church, as they had asked and believed they had received the forgiveness of their Lord and Master, Jesus Christ.

Many Chinese Christians who denied their Lord during the uprising afterwards confessed their sin and returned to the Church, a Church that rejoiced that 'so many were strong enough to lay down their lives for Christ's sake, and has come forth from the fiery trial, chastened and subdued, perhaps, but all the purer and richer in the divine life for the experiences they have passed through'.

Some of the most moving documents in Christian history are those letters and diaries written by missionaries as they faced death at the hands of the Boxers.

"We are now in very great danger of losing our lives," wrote W. A. McCurrach of the English Baptist Mission to his mother on July 3, 1900. "This is a sad time for China. If all missionaries are murdered, it will move the Church in a remarkable way. If it is God's way of evangelising China, then surely we ought to be ready to die for the Gospel's sake. None of us want to die, but we all want to say, 'Thy will be done'." Ten days later when twenty-six missionaries, including women and children, had been beheaded, and one of his evangelists had been burned to death, his faith remained undimmed. "This must be God's way of purifying the Church and making sure of its final success."

An American missionary with the Christian and Missionary Alliance shortly before his death wrote: "Our way to the coast is cut off. Tell all our friends we live and die for the Lord. The

Catholics are preparing to defend themselves, but it is vain. We do not like to die with weapons in our hands; if it be the Lord's will, let them take our lives."

There were missionaries with babies.

"We found the road very hard to travel, over the steep, rough mountains," a Swedish mother wrote. "In the heat, thirst parched us; I could walk only a little way and then sink down exhausted. Our baby's eyes were inflamed by the heat, and he suffered very much. But we had a small enamelled saucepan and a bottle of water, so by preparing him some condensed milk, which we had still, and native arrowroot, we kept him alive."

Sometimes her husband was in awful agony of pain from hunger, but when she spoke to him about it he said, "It is no matter when we suffer for Jesus' sake. I rejoice that through these sufferings the Church will be awakened into new life. The field is being watered with blood, and what a harvest there will be!"

When her husband died, she wrote, "God wonderfully comforted me, and to my heart came with power these words, heard long ago outside the gate of Nain, 'Weep not . . .' On December 6 the Lord gave me a little daughter, sound in body and mind; which was another of God's great mercies, seeing what I had passed through."

There came an official settlement of the Boxer uprising, with the wide publication of imperial decrees prohibiting anti-foreign societies. Compensation was offered. Hudson Taylor decided to seek compensation for mission premises and property but later decided that in the light of the great suffering of the Chinese Christians, and to distinguish the missionaries from the representatives of the temporal power and to show to the Chinese the meekness and gentleness of Christians, not only not to enter any claim against the Chinese government but to refrain from accepting compensation even if offered.

Societies which did not share his viewpoint presented their claims and damages were assessed.

Imperial decrees do not, however, change deep-seated attitudes or wipe out memories. After seeing his wife buried, Archibald Glover, in the tradition of the finest missionaries, was able to write: "Was he not granting us the high privilege of knowing in measure the fellowship of the sufferings of his own beloved son? Did he not design by the persecution the purification of his Church in China? And was it not, after all, only what he told us to expect as the appointed portion of all who will to live godly in Christ Jesus and enter the Kingdom of God?"

"I am so glad," said a girl of five, dying after months of captivity with her parents, "I am so glad that I have had to suffer something for Jesus."

Long after the uprising was over fresh stories came to be known of brutality and courage.

Mrs. Howard Taylor in *Guinness of Honan* tells of one Shansi Christian who was weaving when the Boxers suddenly entered her little home.

"Wait a moment till I come down from my loom," she called.

"Deny your faith in Jesus!" they shouted, sword in hand.

Quietly, she went to the cupboard and putting on her best garments, while they watched in surprise, came and knelt down in the midst of them, saying: "Now you may do as you please, for I will not deny my Lord."

Their rage hastened her to the presence of God.

The uprising was at its height at the time of Yu-teh's birth. The previous year, on June 25, 1899, a proclamation had been posted up at the telegraph office at T'aiyuen Fu, the headquarters of Boxerism, which warned:

Foreign religions are reckless and oppressive, disrespectful to the gods and oppressive to the people. The Righteous People will burn and kill. Your judgments from Heaven are about to come. Turn from the heterodox and revert to the truth. Is it not benevolence to exhort you people of the Christian religion? Therefore reform early. If you do your duty, you are good people. If you do not repent there will be no opportunity for after-regret. For this purpose is this proclamation put forth. Let all comply with it.

A Methodist missionary said in some areas it was enough to

possess a box of matches (foreign fire) or a Western book, or umbrella, or pair of shoes, to be connected with a missionary, or any other foreigner, for a Chinese to lose his life.

By Yu-teh's eighth birthday the atrocities were becoming a memory, but the distrust of foreigners lingered, particularly in the villages. The foreigner was still 'a setter forth of strange gods', and his presence was blamed for lack of rain, the dusty earth, and times of famine.

"Let all the various foreign devils be banished from our land," men still whispered.

Missionary doctors were still suspected of removing the eyes and hearts of orphan children for making foreign medicine. Peasants were frightened of the Bible because of foreign devils ink which had to be kept away from their eyes. Similarly they covered their noses and their mouths with their long sleeves to stop foreign influence entering them when a missionary approached. Even the railway was thought to facilitate the spread of various invisible evil influences.

In Yu-teh's village there was antipathy against the railway because it cut ruthlessly through the sacred places where the dead were buried. Because there were no communal burying grounds each family buried on his own plot of land.

Yu-teh was aware of the hatred of the foreign religion as he watched a Chinese pastor, his wife and three children move in to the empty courtyard in his village and hang out their sign advertising Christian services once a week.

The village expressed its alarm, fearing that the gods would punish them for sheltering the foreign religion. The gods' displeasure would mean sickness or even death.

It was plain to Yu-teh, little boy though he was, that action should be taken to carry out the wishes of his neighbours, and drive the new family out.

He spoke to other children in the village, but when they proved hesitant, he went forth alone to tackle these eaters of the foreign religion. At a distance. He waited until one of the pastor's sons came out of the courtyard to play, then threw a barrage of stones. His aim was not good, but the son ran screaming into the courtyard. His father appeared and Yu-teh decided on a rapid, if temporary retreat.

"I ran for all I was worth up a passage, then found there was no way through. Their father looked so big, that I was really frightened. I was trapped in a doorway. Then their mother appeared and I was even more terrified. She came up to me and I shrank into the wall. I expected abuse if not blows."

Women in his village were largely confined to their homes, their feet bound, and they hobbled forth only on high days, but not the pastor's wife. He hardly dare look at her face, but she was smiling.

"I am sorry my little boy has been rude to you," she said softly, and he could hardly believe his ears. Surely, she knew. "You would not have thrown a stone at him if he had not been. Come along with me and I will make my little boy apologise."

To the young aggressor's amazement both the pastor and his wife, bowing and folding their hands in an apology, insisted that he join them in their home for some refreshment.

Seeing escape was impossible he decided to accept, taken aback by this unexpected situation.

She took my hand and led me into their home. The first thing I saw was one of her children playing what I later learned was a harmonium. I stared at him making music. I could hardly believe it. The boy I had stoned said how sorry he was and his mother insisted that we became friends. Soon I was climbing on to the *k'ang*, and enjoying two or three cakes of pressed walnuts.

He so appreciated their hospitality that when they asked him to return next First Day for Sunday school, he wanted to accept. He ran home and begged his parents to let him go. He had had his first glimpse of a Christian home. On Sunday he was there, the first of many, many visits. School was a noisy place. The more noise the better the work being done, but it was there he learned to know the pastor's family, and love their kindly ways.

One day he told the pastor that he wanted to become a

Christian. It was a big decision for although only eight he knew how his parents and the whole village would react. At night when he should have been sleeping he had thought of the consequences, and he wanted the pastor and his family to be the first to know. The pastor's reaction was not encouraging.

"How can you possibly become a Christian?" he asked.

Yu-teh was bewildered.

"Do you tell lies?" the pastor demanded.

"Yes," he nodded miserably. "I'm a champion liar."

"Then you cannot be a Christian for the Bible says we must not lie."

He hung his head.

"Do you steal?"

"Yes."

"Do you obey your parents?"

"Not always."

"The Bible says that children must obey their parents."

Yu-teh was much distressed.

"I never knew how wrong it was to do these things, but please I do really want to become a Christian."

The wise pastor took down his Bible and showed the boy how to start by repenting of sin and accepting the forgiveness of Christ. He did not hurry but took him from one Bible passage to another, and then they prayed. Yu-teh who had come to love the Jesus Way because of the example set by these Christians became the first convert in the village. Years later at university he was to be called Stephen.

The time came when the pastor began dropping in at the father's little store, making purchases of farm produce, and getting acquainted with the family and customers. Stephen, as I will now call him, attended the small day school in the village which was managed by the elders, but the pastor suggested to his father that a scholar so bright as his son was deserving of a chance in the mission boarding school in the great city of Peking, at the end of the railway.

In the autumn, at the beginning of the school year, when he was twelve, Stephen found himself a passenger on the 'little fast train' with his father, going to Peking, to enrol. He had ambition and showed industry and he went up and up, through all the subjects, including English, and completed middle school, lower and upper.

During these years he was influenced by Miss Lily Armitt, who had gone to China with the former Foreign Missionary Society of the United Methodist Church. She had come fresh from mission work in London's East End. Years later, when she had retired, he was to know her in England.

He took seriously the observance of morning chapel and Sunday worship, as well as voluntary class-meetings. These activities which seemed burdensome to casual students appealed to him as an opportunity to develop spiritually. Soul growth became a reality.

While he was studying a message came that his mother was seriously ill. He had real affection for her. He returned to the village but as he entered the gate of the courtyard he was told she was dead, and had already been clothed in the embroidered costume that families put on their dead.

He refused to believe it could be possible. When others in the home had made it hard for him because he was a Christian he had known she loved him. He went into the room and found her face covered with a cloth.

"I want my mother. God, I want my mother," he cried.

The mourners rushed in to comfort him, casting a glance at the body on the bed. As they looked her head moved. In a barely audible voice she asked for a drink. She was not dead after all. Stephen's cry of anguish turned to one of astonishment and praise.

2

The Student

WITH A SCHOLARSHIP to the Yenching university Stephen was seen by various missionaries as a future Methodist pastor. He did not dismiss the idea, it appealed for a variety of reasons, but he would not commit himself. There seemed so many openings in this new world which centred in Peking. The Republic of China had been formally established, on January 1, 1912. It was based on the Three Principles of the People: Nationalism, Democracy and Social Well-being. The objective was Chinese independence and freedom.

There were three Christians in the cabinet. In April 1913 they sent a telegram to provincial officials and Church leaders throughout the land:

"Prayer is requested for the National Assembly now in session; for the newly established government; for the President yet to be elected; for the Constitution of the Republic; ... that peace may reign ... that strong virtuous men may be elected as officials, and that the government may be established on a firm foundation ... Let us all take part."

The world newsagency Reuter commented: "This is the first time in the history of the world that such an appeal has come from a non-Christian nation ... a striking proof of the deep changes that are being accomplished in China by the Revolution."

Stephen gave himself with impassioned vigour to his studies, and although he did not always like what his tutors taught, he showed a pleasant courtesy, and an application which won him approval. But sometimes, impatient for change, he questioned why foreigners exercised so much authority in the Church and university, and longed for the day when the Chinese would be in control.

In books and debates with other students he had been influenced by wild talk of missionary imperialism. Previously, he had seen the missionaries as benefactors, bringing education and healing as well as their faith in Christ, to China. He had liked those whom he had known personally, but here was a new angle. While studying in their premises he could be a rebel.

The American writer, Edgar Snow, has written that to educated Chinese the arrival of missionaries was always associated with China's military defeats. While the statement contained some truth, Stephen read in 1922 of the National Christian Conference in Shanghai, where the majority of the 1,200 delegates were Chinese. The chairman was also Chinese; these delegates issued the following statement:

We express our appreciation of the work of the missionaries, who through untold difficulties have blazed the way and laid down the great structure for national evangelisation, and our gratitude to the Christian Churches of the West, through whose faithful support the missionary work had been developed and attained its present growth.

We Chinese Christians declare that we have the commission from the Head of the Church, Jesus Christ, to proclaim the Gospel to every creature.

We confidently hope that the time will soon come when the Church in China will repay in part, for that which she has bountifully received from her mother Churches in the West, the loving tributes of the daughter ... contributions in thought, life and achievements, for the enrichment of the Church catholic.

Stephen by no means lived in a critical mood, for as he read and discovered the variety of life in a great city, as he listened to the lecturers and the preachers in chapel, both Western and Chinese, he dreamed of the future and in his prayers recalled the Chinese pastor who had come to his village.

There were ten thousand other villages to which he might have gone. Why had God sent him to his village?

His family were Buddhists, he was a Christian, but in his classes he learned about other religions in China, and was attracted by Confucius. He saw Confucianism more as a philosophy than a dynamic life-changing force like Christianity, but its progression from the head to the heart, from being to doing and from the immediate to the distant, appealed to his mind.

There was considerable peasant poverty in the villages, and in Peking the students had barely sufficient, but it did not matter that clothes were old when everyone was similarly placed. The wealth they sought was education.

Another young man, Mao Tse-tung, born in 1893, in a small village in Hunan province, was developing and rebelling. The objective of his rebellion was his father, an ex-soldier who had become a rich peasant, who regularly beat his children to make them obedient. Both mother and father were uneducated.

In a blazing row with his father when he was thirteen Mao threatened to kill himself. His mother ran after him as he stood on the edge of a pond ready to jump in. His father, cursing, commanded him to come back. Mao agreed if his father promised not to beat him.

"Thus the war ended and from it I learned that when I defended my rights (dignity) by open rebellion my father relented but when I remained meek and submissive he only cursed and beat me the more. Reflecting on this, I think that in the end the strictness of my father defeated him. I learned to hate him."

Meanwhile Stephen studied his college books, listened to his teachers, and wondered if Christianity could ever be accepted in China as in other countries.

Each summer the more mature students in Yenching university were given a stipend sufficient to provide for physical needs, and assigned to pastors of churches or chapels, who would guide them in work with young people. Stephen took eagerly to the arrangement. He was extremely conscientious in the discharge of his duties, even to preaching the Sunday morning sermon.

One summer he was sent to Ching-hsien on the new Tientsin-Pukow railway. He found the church much run-down. Although there were many names on the church-roll, the Sunday congregation had dwindled to the point that only a school-teacher, the chapel-keeper and the pastor showed up for worship. He saw the situation as a scandal.

He spruced himself up with a fresh cotton gown and began to call on all the local notables, the postmaster and his letter carriers, the railway station-master, and the clerical staff, the merchants and their apprentices, the principal of the higher primary school and his staff, and even — most difficult of all — the local gentry, stiff with pride and starched with prejudice.

On the theory that if he could capture the élite the rest would follow, he made up his mind to tackle the autocrat of the local scholars, the crustiest of the Confucian élite. It was a bold idea, which nearly miscarried. He called on a boiling hot afternoon when the servants were drowsing in their corners and the scholar was sipping tea over a musty book of morals, seated on the k'ang. Not a breath stirred the sultry atmosphere. Nothing daunted, Stephen rattled the gate-bolt, in lieu of a bell, called up the gatekeeper and handed in his red visiting card. The gate-keeper disappeared. After a long interval he returned, and waved him in with bad grace.

The scholar evidently felt the need of an infusion of new thought, and was prepared for diversion by this upstart student from Peking. But Stephen, qualified by courage out of the ordinary to bear the name of the first Christian martyr, was not willing to pass up an opportunity to witness for his Master. He came to the point of his interview at once, and with enthusiasm, stating the claims of Christ.

When he realised what was happening the old man was speechless with indignation. Then recovering himself he roared at the top of his voice, "Quick, call the dogs! Put him out! How came you to let this Jesus doctrine fanatic into my presence? Out with him this instant!"

The servants and the dogs came running, and the outlook was dark for Stephen, but at that very moment, in came the station-master from the railway. The station-master, a person of some note in the community with access to all the best homes, had a twinkle in his eye, having taken in the situation at a glance.

"So, my friend," he declared, addressing the scholar, "you have been fortunate enough to have a visit from the young minister from Peking. Our town is indeed favoured to have such a distinguished teacher spend the summer in our midst. There is not a better informed person. He has all the latest scientific information at his finger-tips, and as for his character and patriotism he is without a peer. But what are these dogs doing here?" And lifting his stick, he chased them out of the room.

The intervention came not a moment too soon. Stephen found himself elevated to a place of honour before the whole family. He could only thank God in silence for the unexpected deliverance, and mustered his dignity to take leave of the flustered scholar and bow to his heaven-sent friend.

The gateman who let him out at the great gate, bowed low in honour, and wondered at the change in status accorded to the young evangelist. It would be pleasant to say that the scholar became a Christian, but there is no evidence of this. But that summer, while Stephen spent a few days in Anshan with his family, he saw his father turn to Christ, a step in bringing the entire family to God.

During these years there was revolution, bloodshed and devastation in large areas of China, but it was also a period when the Church was attracting more support, not least from those who sought Western knowledge. Americans in particular were providing the resources for schools, hospitals and colleges. But there were problems.

The Rev. H. B. Rattenbury, Methodist chairman of the Wuchang District, wrote in 1922 that the Church in China was still seen to be a foreign thing. A survey of the Christian occupation of China had revealed that there were 130 separate Protestant societies propagating Christianity, each with its own home-board and organisation, and its denominational affinities and loyalties.

"These multitudinous divisions are the masks of a foreign Church," he wrote. "The Chinese Christian conscience will have none of them."

Stephen was numbered among that conscience, and he joined in the discussions about a Chinese Home Missionary Society which aimed to give expression to the missionary consciousness of the whole Protestant Church of China. He shared the view that the old division of the Western Church should not continue long in China, but the problem was that the Christians in the West preferred to support denominational activity.

Stephen secured a B.A. and B.D. at Yenching university, and commenced post-graduate studies. At this period he met the lovely girl who was to be his wife. She was also studying at the university and was in charge of extra-curricular activities. In those days few Chinese girls had the opportunity of a university education and those who did were from wealthy families.

The president of the university was Dr. John Leighton Stuart, a missionary educator from America, who had largely brought the university into being.

Dr. Stuart had been born in Hangchow, China, of missionary parents. As a child and young man he had an aversion for missionary life, but after his graduation he returned to China as a missionary and remained for nearly fifty years.

Yenching university had the highest academic standards, but was an integral part of missionary enterprise. There were no compulsory religious services, but Dr. Stuart believed that proper university standards and an avowed Christian purpose were not incompatible. Within the university was a strong Christian fellowship, also a school of religion, primarily for college graduates. Although American financial support had made possible the establishing of the university, the aim from the start was that this should be essentially a Chinese university.

It was five miles from Peking, located in what had been the ruined garden of a Manchu prince. Dr. Stuart restored the landscaping of the garden and it became to be described as the most beautiful campus in the world.

One day Stephen was invited to speak in the women's

section of the university, which was segregated and watched over by the dean of women. He gladly accepted but was rather conscious of his appearance for smallpox had left his face lightly pitted. It accounted for his appealing shyness, and possibly a desire to excel in his studies more than his contemporaries. He was much sought after, in spite of his shyness, possibly because he was regarded as an outstanding student destined for leadership.

The girl students, many of whom were training as church workers, flattered him, praised his speech, and invited him back again. He was in excellent spirits. The dean of women, known to the girls as older sister, was impressed by him, and on a subsequent visit she spoke to him of one of her brightest girls whom she was aware he had noticed.

"I saw you glancing at her."

"I admire her very much," he blushed. "She is so talented and beautiful. If she did not come from such an excellent family . . ."

"If you are interested in her, I think she would like to meet you," said the dean. "Shall I arrange this?"

It was the first of many meetings, always in the presence of this discerning woman, and soon they both knew they were in love. Open courtship was difficult, and indeed impossible in old China, but their thoughts were filled with the spring and the flowers and the butterflies, symbols of love with Chinese poets.

Lin Yutang has told in his book *My Country and My People* how the Chinese girl had many ingenious ways of making her presence felt.

The most innocent form was showing one's small red shoes beneath the wooden partitions. Another was standing on the verandah at sunset. Another was accidentally showing one's face amidst peach blossoms. Another was going to the lantern festivals of January and June at night. Another was playing on the *ch'in*, a stringed instrument, and letting the young man in the next house hear it. Another was asking the teacher of her younger brother to correct her poetry, with the younger brother as the messenger boy. The teacher, if he were young and romantic, might send a verse in reply.

Because of the wisdom and good practical sense of the dean of women none of these things were necessary in Stephen's romance. She saw that in spite of his modest background, that her own outstanding student and he would make a fine partnership. She regarded secret meetings as unhealthy, although there were some, but under her gaze she watched their respect and love for each other grow.

There were weeks of anguish. He was anxious about his own humble status, nervous of how her endowed family would receive him, but he did not question her love. Distinguished, upper-class families did not like their children to marry the children of farmers and peasants but, at last, through the traditional match-makers he was given permission to marry. For days he could hardly contain his high-spirits. He just couldn't stop smiling.

Yenching was still small enough for the president to know most of the students by name, and he formed a friendship with Stephen and his friend Philip Fugh. He let it be known that he approved of Stephen's forthcoming wedding. After he had retired Dr. Stuart was to write in his autobiography *Fifty Years in China*, published by Random House, that one of the most beautiful traditions of Chinese life had long been the relation between teacher and pupil.

Every foreigner who has taught Chinese of whatever age or social class can testify to the richness of this experience. It is something more warmly human than mere respect or even veneration on the pupil's part, instinctive and yet delightfully spontaneous. In my first years at Yenching, when the students were few in number and I was still wondering just what a college president really did, it was easy to know each one of them.

The wedding date was fixed near the Chinese New Year in 1926.

Stephen had to travel to her home for the wedding. He went alone as his family were unable to be present. To his relief, he was received kindly not only by the immediate family, but by numerous relations, who respected his scholastic achievements.

No one mentioned the smallpox scars. Polite questions were asked about his family, but no one embarrassed him by probing. But he was short of money. There were so many relations to be visited, each of whom gave free hospitality on a lavish scale, and their servants expected generous gifts from him. Risking misunderstanding, he had to decline invitations, because the families had so many expectant servants.

His education secured him a place which his background might have denied him, and he found himself developing poise and serenity among his well-bred friends. From his attractive wife he studied the social graces, and they were numerous. Their elders approved the match.

Stephen left Yenching and partly at Dr. Stuart's suggestion joined the staff of the Student Volunteer Movement.

In America the Student Volunteer Movement for Foreign Missions recruited college students for missionary service, and Dr. Stuart heard the call to China through its secretaries. The Movement, then at its peak, believed that it was the duty of any Christian young man to show why he should not be a foreign missionary. In China, the Student Volunteer Movement sought to attract choice students to the ministry of the Church. Sometimes it met in the same places as the Marxists.

The headquarters of the Student Volunteer Movement were in Shanghai, and the young couple travelled from Peking to make their first home there. Alongside its aggressive glamour, the foreign business-houses and hotels, and its glittering riches, they viewed the slums and watched the beggars outside the opium dens and gambling clubs. Stephen assisted the head of the Movement, and found his duties immensely rewarding and his new life satisfying. He travelled within the eighteen provinces within the Great Wall, visiting the Christian institutions from which the Protestant churches hoped to draw their pastors and evangelists.

Although it seemed probable that he would be ordained to the Methodist ministry, it was not to be; rather in future years he would be described as the number one Methodist Chinese layman.

It was already apparent that he was not a good committee man. He wanted to forge ahead while others patiently deliberated, but his work prospered. Patience is one of the nobler virtues of the Chinese: there is a saying, 'A man who cannot tolerate small ills can never accomplish great things'.

He made a few senior colleagues angry. He was not as submissive as they wished, even appearing arrogant in attitude, but they were wise enough not to wish to destroy the virile, self-confident individualism which when matured would fit him for leadership. He belonged to a generation that would not be exploited.

His love for the Methodist Church was intense. In later years he spoke with devotion of Christ rather than the Church, and of Christ's excellence, but he never forgot it was the Methodist Church which showed Christ to him.

As a class, missionaries, he found, were like any other group of people, wise and foolish, selfless and selfish, but Stephen was to look back with inexpressible gratefulness to those pioneers who had touched his life, one or two of whom he had sadly misjudged. It seemed to be part of their calling to be misunderstood, like their Master.

The experienced missionaries knew that the Holy Spirit would do his own work in the development of Stephen, a young man of strong personality, of whom astonishing things were expected. Academically, he was advanced, but he had yet to absorb into his experience the words of Jesus: "I tell you truly that unless a grain of wheat falls into the earth and dies, it remains a single grain of wheat; but if it dies, it brings a good harvest. The man who loves his own life will lose it, and the man who hates his life in this world will preserve it for eternal life."

3

The Headmaster

AT TWENTY-NINE Stephen was offered the headship of Tangshan Methodist school, in the North China District, near Peking. There were both day boys and boarders. It was a considerable opportunity, but was he equipped for the position? As always he turned to his wife who had majored in education. She was well-fitted for a headmaster's wife and those responsible for the school had no doubt considered this.

She had great faith in Stephen and suggested that he find out more. She had not overlooked that as a headmaster he would not be away from home for such long periods.

Tangshan was a large, industrial town, a mining and railway centre, and the base of the Methodist Hopei sub-district. It was surrounded by endless plains, and plagued by constant wind and dust storms. In the commercial offices were Chinese who had studied abroad. The Methodist school had a board of directors, representing the administration and industry of the town. It had a fine reputation.

Stephen met the directors and all was set fair for his appointment when the question of salary arose. It was the custom for Chinese national workers to be paid less than their missionary colleagues. He refused to accept this, insisting on being treated the same as Europeans or Americans. The directors adjourned, rather put out.

Stephen went home and told his wife.

They both prayed and spent several fretful days, then word came that he had been appointed at full salary. Friends showered their congratulations on him, including the directors who bore no ill-will, but trusted he would be as firm when the welfare of the school was at stake. He was, as they quickly found.

Late at night when the boys slept, the light burned in his study as he mapped new classrooms and dormitories. There was no reason he could see, apart from funds, why the school should not double, treble in size, when schools were so few. And he would not be limited by finance.

Stephen's appointment as headmaster was, no doubt, influenced by new Nationalist Movement regulations which had been introduced following violent anti-foreignism and intense missionary persecution in 1925. About forty per cent of missionaries left China.

The new regulations compelled foreign educational institutions, including those of missions, to be Chinese in administration. Presidents and heads of all colleges were to be Chinese. Christianity could no longer be a compulsory subject in the higher grades of school and was banned altogether from primary schools. The new regulations resulted in the rapid development of Sunday schools.

The Methodists congratulated themselves on having someone so admirably equipped as Stephen and there was no reluctance about his appointment.

In 1933, the Rev. Harold Rattenbury, a Methodist superintendent, visited Tangshan, and reported to the Methodist Missionary Society in London that there were now four hundred boys of whom two hundred were boarders. He found that the school had attained a popularity never before reached in all its history, and that a Methodist doctor who had prospered had given £800 for the erection of the buildings.

"Amongst those four hundred lads," he wrote, "there is a wonderful opportunity for Christian work. To see them gathering for morning assembly, and to have the privilege of talking to them of the Christian way of life, is a great experience."

Stephen was impressed with the statesmanship of the

Methodist superintendent, and found they both shared a desire to see a distinct Chinese emphasis in prayers, services of worship, in architecture for church buildings and in theology. In preserving the truths of Christianity China's ancient civilisation should not be ignored.

In later years he would quote T. C. Chao's thoughts on an indigenous church: "It will be entirely supported by Chinese money, wholly governed by Chinese Christians, completely reorganised to suit the Chinese genius, and freely enriched by Chinese thought."

In 1933, however, there was still considerable dependence on support from overseas, but Stephen found there were wealthy Chinese businessmen who would contribute to the school. When the directors tried to restrain him because there were no funds, he would persuade these businessmen to lend their money. After he had borrowed it he would persuade them to give it, and because he had many friends the school grew and its reputation was established throughout China.

His own children did not go to school until they were ten, his wife teaching them at home. They were bright children and both the eldest son and eldest daughter entered medical college at sixteen.

In the 1930s floods and famine troubled China as Chiang Kaishek endeavoured to suppress the Communists. Peasants crowded into the big cities in search of food, many dying of cold and hunger. In Shanghai hired carts crawled round the streets at dawn collecting the dead. Meanwhile, the Japanese army occupied Manchuria.

Mao saw his opportunity to lead the peasant in a major revolution. In his *Report of an Investigation into the Peasant Movement*, he wrote:

"The force of the peasantry is like that of raging winds and driving rain. It is rapidly increasing in violence. Every revolutionary comrade will be subject to their (the peasants) scrutiny and will be accepted or rejected by them. Shall we stand in the vanguard and lead them, or stand behind them and oppose them?"

While Mao hated the landlords, his soldiers allegedly were

forbidden to take a needle from a peasant's house without paying for it, and had to labour on any farm where they were billeted. Landlords were robbed and frequently killed, their land being re-allocated under Communist guidance.

Stephen wondered about the fate of his school if the Communists occupied Tangshan, but in 1934 the Red Armies were on the retreat, a retreat which was to become known as the Long March. It began in the autumn with ninety thousand men and a few women. In twelve months they were to walk six thousand miles, crossing mountains and rivers, taking their prisoners with them. The pass over one mountain was sixteen thousand feet high, the temperature below freezing, and many of the soldiers were barefoot. Thousands died from exposure, exhaustion and fever. Only seven thousand men and thirty women finally arrived in Yenan, Shensi, but Mao had established himself as supreme leader.

Among the prisoners of the Red Armies were two C.I.M. missionaries.

One of these missionaries, Alfred Bosshardt, travelled thousands of miles, mostly on foot, being billeted in some three hundred places. In the winter his clothes were frozen stiff, and the mane of the horses bristled with icicles. In the summer the sweat ran off him as the sun burned down.

When they were pursued by aircraft he had to take cover several times a day, but the opportunity to escape did not occur. Few of the soldiers were members of the Communist Party proper, which held meetings for members only. There were halts for executions. When he was present he looked away, until the beheaded victims had been thrown into the river.

When Mr. Bosshardt asked his captors why they had become Red soldiers they replied, "Because we were hungry", but on the Long March they ran short of food, two meals being supplied instead of three, the first being of rice gruel and the second of steamed rice eaten with vegetables or a tiny portion of meat. There were days when they had only one meal, mainly corn.

There were constant negotiations, as well as prayers, for his release, his companion by now being free.

Mr. Hermann Becker asked the Communists why they arrested missionaries. Sometimes it was to obtain huge ransoms, but primarily he was told it was because 'the teachings of non-resistance and of man's dependence on a higher being are contrary to the Communist doctrine'.

Alfred Bosshardt was released, very ill, on Easter Sunday, 1936. He had been a prisoner for eighteen months. He went home to England to recover, but later returned to China and was among the last missionaries to leave in 1951.

"Your faith held?" Stephen asked him years later.

"Nightly, my pillow was: 'In peace will I both lay me down and sleep; for Thou, Jehovah, alone makest me dwell in the land of safety'."

While the Tangshan school developed so did the attacks on Christianity. Stephen made it his duty, and that of his staff, to study the thinking behind these intellectual offensives.

The Great Federation of Non-Religionists were circulating anti-religion propaganda. Their attack was threefold. On religion itself, as being an out of date product of primitive people unfavourable to human progress. On Christian teaching, as being unscientific, contrary to logic and social theories. On the Church, for its support of capitalism, its 'sin against the national integrity of the Chinese people', and the low moral standards of rice Christians.

However by 1937 in China thirteen Christian universities had been founded, 260 Christian middle schools, with over fifty thousand students, and thousands of primary schools.

On Easter Day 1937, the Chinese press which had so often filled its pages with abuse about Christianity came out with headlines: 'Chiang speaks of the sufferings of Jesus'. There were those who said, 'The Lord is risen indeed.'

In July of that year there was a fresh twist in the story of the Chinese Church: the Sino-Japanese war. As the Japanese invaders advanced the capital was moved from Peking to Chungking in the interior, 1,400 miles from the coast. But the Methodist school in Tangshan and Yenching university in Peking could not move and studies continued for months unhindered. At this point Japan was not at war with England or America and the missionaries were in a position to assist their Chinese brethren.

The degree of suffering in China was beyond imagination. By December 1941 it was calculated that six million Chinese soldiers had been killed or wounded. There were fifty million refugees. The cost of living in some occupied areas had risen by one thousand per cent.

In 1939 there was widespread intimidation of Chinese Christians, and entire congregations found themselves being driven away from Sunday services for questioning. Most were released but some were bound and beaten, or tortured for information.

The Church opened camps for refugees, and hundreds of thousands passed through them. The Chinese Christians adapted the Psalm to read: 'The Lord is our refugee camp, a very present help in trouble.'

There were a few Christians among the Japanese soldiers and they were free to attend Chinese Church services. Mission hospitals were overcrowded caring for hundreds of casualties.

The worst atrocities were often committed by the advancing soldiers before the arrival of their senior officers who, at least in theory, had a code of conduct. Women were raped, homes looted, and men beaten.

To stop the advancing enemy railway lines were destroyed, fields flooded, factories burned down. Forty million people were homeless or subject to extreme poverty. Churches became cinemas for Japanese troops and millions migrated to west China.

Students trekked up to one thousand miles to continue their studies in freedom.

Stephen watched the great exodus; the wheelbarrows which threatened to collapse beneath their load of household goods; the weary mothers carrying their young; the older women, with bound feet, who like the sick were completely dependent on others. Goats and sheep were crowded into trains with bedding and people trying to get away before the enemy arrived. When the carriages would not take another thing, the adventurous clambered on to the carriage roofs. The scenes were unbelievable.

It was difficult for Christians to know whether to join the trek from the Occupied Zone to Free China. Church leaders who went were charged with cowardice, while those who remained were suspected of collaboration.

Stephen knew his place was at Tangshan which because of its Western connection enjoyed some immunity. Some students had fled, but most remained. Then, overnight, the situation changed on December 7, 1941. Missionaries in occupied China heard the news with unbelief.

"The Japs have attacked the American fleet at Pearl Harbour."

"They wouldn't dare."

Soon there was confirmation from every Japanese soldier who boasted of the immobilised American Pacific Fleet.

"America's declared war on Japan."

"So has Britain and the Dominions."

Word went along the corridors of the school, from classroom to classroom. Stephen called the staff together for an emergency meeting as Free China joined the British and American Commonwealths in alliance against the Japanese. A mission school was obviously high on the Japanese list of priorities.

Not for the first time Stephen found himself saying, "God is our refuge and help". Some students were already missing from their classrooms, detained at home by their parents. To be a headmaster was to be in a very hot seat, but most of the staff rallied round loyally.

Within hours a Japanese officer arrived.

"This school is now under the control of Great Japan," he said, and no one argued.

Japanese soldiers triumphantly marched into the grounds.

There was an abrupt hardening of attitudes towards anything American or British. 'Enemy nationals' were instructed to wear bright red armbands, with a registration number and a letter — A for the Americans; B for the British; N for the Norwegians, and X for all other unfriendly nations.

Dr. Stuart was arrested, but while many were sent to camps he was kept under guard locally with two other men. A young Norwegian missionary somehow managed to cook a meal for them on Saturday nights.

Overseas support for Tangshan school, Yenching university, and similar educational establishments and churches ceased. Chinese pastors experienced poverty and tribulation, but they did not desert their churches. The Japanese constantly found fault with mission schools, hospitals, and pastors. An instruction was given that the latter had to hand in their written sermons for censorship before they preached them, and had to bow to the Japanese Emperor when they had meetings. The instruction was largely ignored, and some Chinese pastors such as Wang Ming-tao refused to join the Chinese Christian Federation organised by the Japanese.

In 1942 the Japanese launched their Three All Campaign; Burn All, Loot All, Kill All. The campaign was aimed at those peasants who had supported the guerillas, but the Japanese were not always selective, and many who were innocent lost their lives or their possessions. Others fled from the oppression and joined the Communists in Free China.

With the missionaries interned, facing poverty and persecution, the Church might have declined, but the opposite happened, particularly in country districts.

Laymen like Stephen became preachers. Young Chinese men and women travelled from village to village preaching the Gospel with enthusiasm. Those who could paid their own expenses, and those who had nothing went forth in faith.

One young man arrived in Tangshan in the cold winter, with no suitable clothing, but preached with conviction and power.

"Don't you feel cold?" a member of the congregation asked him after the service.

"No," he replied. "I have fire inside."

And it shone from his eyes.

In the absence of the missionaries the Chinese experienced a new sense of responsibility. It was up to them. "Ye that thirst, come to the water: and ye that have no money, come, and buy and drink without money," they declared.

One of Stephen's students named Kao had always been antagonistic towards the faith. Stephen had frequently reasoned with him, without success, but he accepted an invitation to attend a revival meeting. Instead of preaching, however, the lay preacher asked the congregation to kneel and pray together. Annoyed, Kao moved towards the door, but the preacher grasped him.

"If you pray, the grace of God may come upon you," he said.

Unwillingly, the student knelt with the preacher. No words were spoken, but Kao soon started to weep, then cried out loudly, "God forgive me. I am the greatest of sinners."

His parents and his brothers were baptised, and he himself became a local preacher.

In a village near Tangshan where there had been no Christian witness before the occupation, about fifty families became Christians.

"God is compensating for the absence of our missionary brethren with an outpouring of the Holy Spirit," Stephen said. "The heavens are opening. Christianity is again dependent upon God and a lay movement."

"This is God at work," inexperienced Christians confessed as they saw the outcome of their simple witness. "I stumbled and faltered as I spoke."

Some suffered for their witness. One lay preacher on returning home was arrested and shot in prison for it was alleged that he had been away spying, not preaching.

For Stephen there were good days and bad.

With fixed bayonets the Japanese military police arrived at the school and pushed their way to his study.

"You're under arrest," the captain snapped. "Get your things."

It was no shock for his students had expressed anger towards the Japanese. From where he was standing he could see them with the staff being paraded outside. Pride filled him as he saw their quiet orderliness, their lack of panic, but when he was marched in front of them he saw their grave faces.

"It's goodbye for a while," he told himself, "and by the end of the war some of you will have grown up or been shot."

He was taken to a small wooden building, and left alone for several hours, a heavy-booted soldier with bayonet outside the door. He sat up as voices approached. The door opened and he was taken before an officer who questioned him about the staff, the students, and the school routine. It was a slow process, through an interpreter as the officer spoke only Japanese and Stephen spoke only a few words in Japanese.

"Have you anything further to say?" the officer invited with mock courtesy.

Stephen summoned his courage and pointed sharply to the Japanese soldier by his side.

"Isn't this man rather dirty and untidy for a representative of the Emperor?" he asked. He stared directly at his interrogator as the words were interpreted.

The officer was astounded by the impudence and the soldier reddened. Stephen was swiftly dismissed and marched back to the wooden building, but later was recalled. While the soldier had been a disgrace to his uniform, he had insulted a soldier of the Emperor.

"You're absolutely right," a subdued officer confessed. "The escort was untidy. Because the Chinese must have no reason to despise the Japanese he is being returned to Japan at once. It is necessary that you respect us." There was a silence. "Now you are going to be released."

Stephen resisted a reply which would further distress the officer, hardly able to believe he was going back to his school, but the welcome was overwhelming. In the morning assembly there was real thanksgiving.

Months passed. He was in a country inn with a party, including women wearing jewellery, when armed Japanese soldiers burst in. While they searched the guests in one room he suggested the women remove their jewels and give them to him. They were reluctant, believing he would dispose of them, but he feared the soldiers might arrest the women to get possession.

"Do you wish to perish with your gold and silver?" he whispered, getting impatient. They removed the pieces and handed them to him. With seconds to spare he threw it all under a cupboard by the wall. The soldiers stamped in and searched everyone, but when they found nothing of value they left, and the jewellery was restored to its owners.

Stephen, like every Chinese Christian, wanted to give practical aid to the missionaries in occupied China. In 1942 there were about 1,500, half American, the others mainly British. Most were treated considerately, although isolated from the free world, having no radio sets and receiving few letters. The local situation varied from district to district. While in Wuchang the Japanese burned the Anglican Church, in Hangchow the Church Missionary Society carried on its hospital work receiving courteous treatment.

For nearly three years more than ten per cent of the members of the China Inland Mission, together with school children of the Mission, were in Japanese internment camps. Again, it was part of the cost which they, like their predecessors, had to pay for evangelism in China.

Stephen joined hundreds of other Chinese Christians in delivering 'comfort' parcels to the camps whenever possible, but it was a ministry which had to be exercised with caution. The giving was always sacrificial. At Tangshan students complained of hunger and the food was sometimes riddled with grubs which made it unpalatable. There was little in the Wang's kitchen, and prayers like 'Give us this day our daily bread' took on fresh meaning. Clothes had to be repaired over and over, and winter heating presented acute problems, but somehow life went on and there was laughter.

Mostly, the students sullenly accepted the Japanese presence, but whenever possible they endeavoured to undermine their authority.

Stephen was asked to help nearly forty people, including several Christian women, to reach Free China. At first he refused, the long journey not only meant a hardship, but a prolonged absence from Tangshan. There is uncertainty about the circumstances which made him change his mind, but he finally capitulated and one night they stealthily set forth.

They climbed into the back of a truck, changing their route at regular intervals, to make their destination less obvious. They rattled over the roads, slumping wearily. Two or three who were nervous were tempted to call the whole thing off, the doubt and uncertainty too much, but Stephen was not turning back.

"We're almost at the check-point," he smiled. "Let's stop and pray."

The driver joined them.

They clasped their papers and went on, hoping they would not be stopped, but they saw the soldiers looming ahead, and the driver braked. Nerves were starting to jump again.

Stephen jumped down but neither his explanations nor the papers would satisfy the soldiers, and those in the truck looked bleakly at each other, panic in their eyes, all very tired.

The only hope was in God, and Stephen was inwardly praying as he talked to the soldiers, but he was making no headway. At best it seemed they would have to go back. The balance was tipped against them.

An official sprang forward from the shadows, and stepped in front of Stephen.

"Headmaster Wang," he said.

"Yes, who are you?" Stephen gasped. He did not recognise the man, obviously in charge.

"Headmaster, my son is at your school," the official beamed.

The soldiers stepped back. Without further discussion the party was waved through.

"As a father pitieth them that fear him," thought Stephen.

The grimness of the times gave Christians bigger opportunities to demonstrate their faith. Roland Rees who spent nineteen years in China wrote of these years in *China Can Take It*:

Those who criticised us in the past have changed their attitude. During this war they have seen something very real lived before their eyes. They have seen honesty, courage, enterprise, co-operation, devotion and self-sacrifice in the lives of their fellow-countrymen who call themselves by the name of Christ. At last many of them see that this is no mere Western religion but a faith for all men that is deeply concerned with the actual life we all have to live together and which turns it into a thing of beauty and strength and love. This is how Christ is coming to China in war-time, and winning his way to the heart of that great people.

V-J day did not seem long after the German defeat. It took Stephen by surprise, an unbelievably joyous surprise.

Yenching university had been used as a Japanese military hospital, but on August 17 Dr. Stuart was summoned to Gendarmerie headquarters. He was shown into the commandant's reception room. The commandant made a short speech regretting that he had been 'inconvenienced' and informing him that he was now at liberty.

The gates of internment camps were opened and the Japanese soldiers either became excessively polite or went underground. There was wild rejoicing and celebrations.

George Scott of the C.I.M. wrote:

The sympathy, generosity and helpfulness of the Chinese Christians both before and during internment found full expression now that peace had come and the stern grip of the Japanese domination had been removed. They were prodigal in their liberality towards their released missionary friends, and proved they had a rare capacity for rejoicing with those who rejoiced. They came to the camps in buses, rickshaws, cars and on foot, their faces alight with joy and their hands full of gifts. Some came intent on carrying off their friends: "We know you have no money, but that does not matter, for we have saved money and food for this day, so you can come to our homes and rest."

The Shanghai Protestant Churches gave a luncheon party for more than four hundred in honour of the missionary internees. At forty tables in the Comluck restaurant in Bubbling Well Road stories of God's goodness were recounted. "It was worth all internment to have been there," was the confession of more than one missionary.

"To be engulfed in such an overflow of Chinese love, to see the spontaneity of their joy," wrote George Scott, "to hear the testimony of God's presence among them, and feel the sincerity of their outspoken desires for a close and continued fellowship of their missionary friends in the great task which faced the whole Church in China — these things thrilled and satisfied the hungry heart of every internee!"

China's war with Japan had lasted eight years. Stephen saw there was much to be done, but had no conception of how little time there was to do it.

4

Farewell China

THE 1937–45 WAR with Japan had left dislocation and great scars across the face of China. The Christian Church remained weak. In 1926 there were 8,325 Protestant missionaries in China. In 1936 it was 6,059. By March 1947, there were only two thousand even after the arrival from America of two special ships.

Stephen viewed the future with hope. In the universities students were responding to the Gospel in a fashion he had never seen in his youth. They were gathering for early morning prayer meetings and Bible study, and with their vision and energy reaching out to other students and local communities. Student leaders even began to speak of revival.

Leslie Lyall, of C.I.M., also working among students, recorded: "God visited the universities; thousands of students found Christ to be the answer to their personal need."

The Methodist Church, desirous to find how the Church had fared under Japanese occupation, sent the Rev. Harold Rattenbury and Hilda Porter back to China. Their tour included a visit to the school at Tangshan, where Stephen and his wife received them thankfully. They learned how Stephen, under suspicion, had been compelled to flee from the Japanese, but had returned in time to take everything back at the Japanese surrender. Until the early hours of the morning they listened to the stories of deliverance.

The school had been completely looted. Everything moveable,

including furniture, and some doors, windows and even floors had been taken, but most of the buildings were intact, except for a burned-down missionary house and a badly damaged second house which had been in the possession of troops.

Stephen had raised and used something like £2,000 in re-equipping the school. When his visitors nodded approvingly he put forward a typical proposal.

"If my friends and I can raise a further £3,000 would the Methodist Church give £3,000 to complete the renovations?" he asked.

"To this we consented," Rattenbury and Miss Porter wrote in a report published by the Methodist Missionary Society. "We consented on condition that his first care should be the school chapel and that he would engage a Chinese religious worker as well as a missionary for evangelism on the staff."

Stephen raised the bulk of his £3,000 in a fortnight, for the school, like its headmaster, had many friends. It now had five hundred scholars, half day boys and half boarders.

To see their bicycles parked in the school shed was an illuminating sight in China [wrote the visitors]. Mr. Wang dreams of a school of one thousand or more boys of whom one-half shall be boarders. This is, for China, an unusual and colossal adventure — a community rather than a Christian school in the strict sense.

The headmaster is a man of very great capacity. The school has won the praise of the local education authority. The conditions for Christian work among the students are much better than are the openings in government schools and universities which have been so attractive to the Church. Here are a religious and social house, a church to hold upwards of three hundred students, a Chinese and a missionary chaplain on the staff.

Moreover the headmaster is himself an earnest and devoted Christian.

At the conclusion of their China tour they felt, speaking of things as a whole, that the Chinese Church seemed like Lazarus after Christ had raised him from the dead.

There he stood, face covered, hands and legs bound tight: what might happen? Mary and Martha were holding one another in fear and growing joy. "There he is, Mary, our brother, alive. Look." Then once more the Master's voice rings out, "Do something, Martha. It isn't enough to say he's alive. Loose him and let him go."

The Church in China is alive, everywhere. In some places like the great Methodist Church in Hong Kong, it's throbbing and actively alive. In others it's alive amongst the ruins and the problems. It's alive in a day of opportunity quite unparalleled in living memory. But, on the whole, it's weak from lack of food, after four days in the tomb.

Many Chinese Christians in executive positions controlled by American missions were during their career given a chance to spend twelve months in the United States. British missions were normally unable to finance such travel, but Mr. Rattenbury and Stephen spoke of the advantages of his spending a year in Cambridge. Mrs. Wang supported the idea, knowing it had been her husband's wish. Separation was never welcome but he would return renewed and enlarged and the school and decades of pupils would benefit.

Mr. Rattenbury made no promise other than to speak to his principals, but the missionary statesman saw that a visit to Britain would create a better understanding between Stephen and the Missionary Society. He sensed that the headmaster resented taking a place secondary to missionaries.

Stephen had always found it difficult to grasp that in the Methodist constitution there is one place for ministers and another for laity. They usually reciprocate quite cordially. Stephen was a layman. He was headmaster of one of the best schools in north China, and there could be no more honourable place: but he had a slight sense of grievance because, as a layman, he was not a member of the Pastoral Session of Synod, though a number of less able (but ordained) Chinese were members.

The Rev. Howard Smith who was in China from 1924 to 1946 had discussed with Stephen the possibility of his ordination. Mr. Smith was the superintendent of the English Methodist Church in north China.

I had to explain to him, [he recalls] that, unlike the American Methodists many of whose headmasters were also Reverend, in the English Methodist Church to which we belonged every man who became ordained had to promise to go wherever he might be sent. If the Church wanted him to leave his present job, he must be prepared to obey. At the time Stephen was not prepared to consider that he might have to relinquish his position as headmaster of Tangshan college. Later, in England he came to accept God's call wherever it might lead.

His unique contribution was the building up of the Tangshan Methodist College. There was no one else who could have done this with the same success. Yet in our younger days he was not easy to work with, and often went his own way in opposition to school committees. He resented the disciplines which were imposed by the Church on its servants. He was ambitious, and sometimes his ambition made him want to run before he had learned to walk. But he was very likeable and friendly.

I think that it was only gradually that Christ was formed in him, and his likeness to Christ grew as he faced the hard challenges and sufferings of life. He had to face bitter trials when Communist agents infiltrated into the school both among staff and students. The frustrations and disappointments made him lean more and more heavily on Christ. I noticed a new note in his letters which spoke of a firm assurance and deeper faith.

He came under the influence of Wang Ming-tao in Peking, and it was the preaching of that evangelist which, I think, changed his life, causing him to give his life to Christ as he had not done before.

Wang Ming-tao was the pastor of Peking's largest church. His ministry had an even wider influence in China than Watchman Nee's. He was born in the same year as Stephen and they attended the same school, then for some years their paths separated. While Stephen travelled for the Student Volunteer Movement, Wang Ming-tao was jobless having been dismissed as a teacher after several incidents including conducting a service of baptism in a river where the temperature was near freezing. Although often hungry his unemployment was no tragedy for he spent the three years in intensive study of the Bible. In what might have been a desert experience he found riches which thousands later shared through his preaching or by reading his quarterly *Spiritual Food*.

Stephen, with a new spiritual hunger, went to the church in Peking when there was opportunity, and sat with the congregation of one thousand, absorbing the Biblical exposition at the feet of his boyhood friend. As he listened his eyes were opened to a heavenly vision, to Christian living which is 'in demonstration of the Spirit and power'.

"What have I been missing?" he asked himself, sharing his thoughts with his wife. Here was liberation for the captives, sight for the blind, liberty for those who are bruised, all to be found in Christ.

For long a phenomenal reader he turned to the Bible as if it were a newly translated book available for the first time to the Chinese. Lighter reading was put aside. In its covers he found wealth indeed, a wealth he had glimpsed afresh in the ministry of Wang Ming-tao. He was no longer concerned with a critical scientific or historical study, that he had undertaken in his youth, but with what God was saying to him through its pages. From a textbook it became a guidebook. He read in the childlike spirit of which Christ speaks and found that his mind and heart were reawakened. Instead of Biblical information he was seeking and finding God.

Life assumed a new reverence. Jesus Christ had not only reshaped history by His death and resurrection, but was reshaping headmaster Wang. There was a new religious impulse in his direction of the school and his colleagues commented among themselves about it, although he said little.

He watched for the letters from London. There were several but, at last, came confirmation of an invitation for him to spend a year or possibly two in England.

Mr. Rattenbury had made an eloquent plea on his behalf at a large Methodist meeting on October 18, St. Luke's Day. An offering had been given towards the cost of his fare.

Stephen was filled with joy and expectancy.

"Did I tell you about my good fortune?" he asked everyone he met. "It seemed so improbable but I'm going to Cambridge."

All his associates knew of Cambridge. It was of no importance that England was recovering from war and still had food rationing. After all, one did not go to Cambridge to eat, and none respect education more than the Chinese.

His family calculated the distance from Tangshan to the university city and back again. Provision was made for his absence at the school, which those in London were now calling a college, and his wife and children busied themselves preparing the essentials he would need to take. It had to be very limited essentials as he was flying.

Excellent progress had been made on renovating and enlarging the school, and the dream of one thousand students was being fulfilled. For headmaster Wang, it seemed, the future was promising. For his wife the separation would be painful.

"You will come back?"

He assured her.

She smiled trustingly, but the next day would need to be relieved again.

"I wish you could come with me."

"Even if we had the money, there's the children . . ."

He looked at her and nodded. What a strength she had been to him since they first met. He could not imagine how life would have shaped without her. She vitalised all she touched.

When the time came for his departure in spring, 1948, he had made all the administrative arrangements necessary for his absence from the school. In the teaching schedule every month was mapped out, special days were planned, and vacations fixed. When he returned structural changes would be complete. Boys and staff gathered in assembly to bid him well, prayers were said, and a hymn sung.

He made an early start to Peking airport, between the single-decker trolleys and the hundreds of cycles which fill Peking's streets from dawn. He looked at the post-war building alongside one-storey houses, some paper-windowed, and the mud lanes within minutes of main highways, and tried to visualise Cambridge. What could England offer to compare with Peking's trips to the Great Wall, the ancient Ming Tombs, the Emperor's Summer Palace, the Temple of Heaven, the zoo and the opera? Soon he would know.

A long line of friends, colleagues, and family formed at the airport departure lounge to see him off. They were all talking simultaneously, with his family the flow of words hiding deeper emotions.

He walked slowly along the line, shaking hands with everyone, his heart beating fast. His wife was at the far end of the line, excited that he was going abroad to widen his education, also sad, but not for a moment wanting to hold him back. It was an honour for him, an honour she and the family shared. By his wife their youngest son, born after a gap of some years, and slightly spoiled by the affection lavished on him. There came the moment to say goodbye. It would have been acceptable for him to shake her by the hand.

But I could not treat her exactly the same [he later recalled], yet in China we do not kiss each other like people do in the West. But I had to show my love, that she was special, so I plucked up my courage and with everyone watching I kissed her.

My small son laughed, but she was happy. I turned and went to the aircraft, which was first going to Shanghai. I did not know that would be the last kiss. Thank God I did not know.

As they rose high above the blanket of white cloud he wished he could see the rural hamlet, not far from an inlet of the Yellow Sea, beside the tracks of the railway, where he had been born. Life in that village had not altered much in two thousand years. The style of the houses, the art of tilling the field, the clothing of the poor, was little different from those of generations of ancestors: except that the Trans-Siberian express went by in that cloud of dust. The customs of the peasants were still regulated by the teachings of ancient sages and by the inscrutable eyes of the idol in the face of the hill at the back of the village.

Now he was crossing the world towards the birthplace of Robert Morrison, Hudson Taylor, and, most of all, John and Charles Wesley. If those two boys had not been saved from the blazing Epworth rectory he would not be on this flight. He knew the story well. On February 9, 1709, a north-east wind whipped the flames until the whole staircase was ablaze. Just before the thatched roof collapsed the last of the children was rescued through a bedroom window. It was John.

"Come neighbours," said Samuel Wesley, as his family stood by the charred timbers of their home, "let us kneel down; let us give thanks to God . . . ; let the house go. I am rich enough."

Stephen knew that ever afterwards John Wesley referred to himself as 'the brand plucked from the burning'. His mother, convinced that he had been preserved for some purpose, wrote: "I do intend to be more particularly careful of the soul of this child, that God has so mercifully provided for."

When he arrived in England he would visit Epworth.

On the flying-boat from Hong Kong he met a titled British lady.

"Since you have your own religions why do you believe in the Western religion?" she asked him. "Your own has so much to offer mankind."

"By Western religion," he replied courteously, as the clouds drifted below, "you mean the Christian faith. But madam, Christianity is not a Western religion."

"It has been Westernised," she said.

He nodded sadly.

"And that Western dress is such a hindrance to its acceptance in large tracts of the world. But tell me, in which religion do you believe?"

"I believe in the Eastern religion," she replied. "It is so much better than ours."

They were soon engaged in deep conversation. He refused to renounce the non-Christian religions, they contained much wisdom, but they knew nothing of the love of God as revealed in Jesus Christ. They discussed Buddhism, Mohammedanism, Confucianism, Taoism and Christianity.

"Mohammedanism and Christianity," he said, "are comparatively new religions in China, and neither has been absorbed into our culture as Buddhism has been. Most Chinese have a faith which includes a mixture of several religions."

The conversation was stimulating and the hours passed, but he did not endeavour to persuade his companion about the Christian way. Stephen the evangelist had not yet been awakened.

5

A Perilous Place

FROM THE AIRPORT Stephen was taken to the London head-quarters of the Methodist Missionary Society where he was treated as a distinguished visitor, meeting ministers and laymen whose names he had known for years. He expressed his gratitude for the generosity which had made it possible for him to cross the world, but because he was realistic and objective he was soon involved in serious discussion.

The new arrival in London often observes what he seeks: historic churches, the Houses of Parliament, big business, red buses, drop-outs, royal parks, over-crowded pavements. Stephen arrived from a headmaster's study looking for advanced educational methods. Unexpectedly, he found on the post-war streets Chinese men and women, struggling to make a living, solely occupied with food and shelter. They were to become a threat and an opportunity.

His destination was Cambridge. Because John Wesley had been at Oxford his dreams had been of that university city, but he soon found Cambridge was one of the loveliest cities in England. He wandered among the ancient colleges, chapels, libraries and sat gazing at the river. What a splendid place to spend one's life.

He missed his own school greatly, and it was humiliating to find that no one, absolutely no one, had heard of Tangshan, so it became easier to say he came from Peking. At least they knew Peking was in China.

"This most beautiful place," he said to himself repeatedly as the seasons changed. Whether autumn, winter, spring or summer, Cambridge was pleasing. How his wife would have loved it. At first his fellow students thought he had a natural shyness, but soon they discovered an unexpected vein of humour, and friendships developed. Until the early hours of a new day he would answer their questions about his country, reminding them that when Britons were primitive pagans China was a world power.

Stephen would have approved what Leslie Lyall wrote:

The Chinese are a great race, perhaps the greatest. China's uniquely long unbroken national history of at least four thousand years makes her the doyen among nations. China, isolated by deserts, mighty mountain ranges, and the wide Pacific, developed the finest culture the world has ever seen — philosophers, poets, painters, architects, craftsmen in porcelain, ivory, gold and silver, encyclopaedists, novelists and dramatists. The Chinese, even the illiterate peasants, have an innate culture; they are a people of great intelligence and enormous industry. In every age they have produced great intellects, great leaders, great generals, great statesmen and recently great scientists.

While he would have believed every word, some in the university would have debated such a view.

In July 1949 came a highlight he would never forget. He was invited to participate in the induction of the Rev. H. B. Rattenbury, as President of the Methodist Conference. The Conference was to take place at the Methodist Central Hall, Liverpool, and his visit to that city was also to give him a new vision for the future.

At the induction service, surrounded by hundreds of Methodist ministers, Stephen, accompanied by the Rev. Jen Li Jen, was privileged to speak. He told how after the last conference the Chinese were full of joy at the news that Mr. Rattenbury, who had laboured in China for thirty-two years, and had since made repeated visits, was chosen as president. Mr. Rattenbury had been a great friend of China and a great helper of her Church, he said.

But the impression he had made could be expressed in Chinese words which could be translated: 'Reverence to God and love of man'. He had established himself by his service. They felt that the Conference had elected a Chinese as president of the Conference. In China they had a homely custom of honouring their leaders by conferring on them a garment. Since it was a practice with the conference, the Chinese Methodists were grateful to the Liverpool District for asking them to present the gown to Mr. Rattenbury.

Stephen's speech caused murmurs of approval throughout the Central Hall.

The ex-President of the Conference stepped forward to confront Mr. Rattenbury:

"In the name of China, as well as this country, I have pleasure in investing you with the Presidential Gown, and handing you Wesley's Field Bible. May you be able to present still more powerfully the Word of God as it is revealed in this book."

In reply the President spoke of the endurance of the Chinese Church.

"It was in the midst of defeat and disaster that in 1939 a Chinese poet and philosopher said to me, 'We shall win. Japan cannot ultimately triumph. Heaven cannot stand such atrocities as are being committed in her name. I can't reason about it. It's a matter of faith.' That was his theology. He believed in a righteous and loving God, who was the framework of his universe."

The *Methodist Recorder* published a photograph of the induction with Stephen standing by the President. He purchased extra copies to send to Tangshan where Mr. Rattenbury's visit was remembered. Through the Conference, as the weekly paper showed, China and Communism were to the forefront. Mr. Rattenbury saw to that.

The President addressed the ministerial session, speaking of perils in the life of a preacher. Stephen, as a layman, was not invited, but afterwards he read the speech, in particular the references to David Hill, an outstanding missionary.

"When David Hill had been in China for seventeen years, at last, a little reluctantly, he returned home to England," Mr. Rattenbury said. "He felt the perils of the pulpit for himself. He had been used to difficulties, to opposition, to rioting and apathy. He saw himself, and others saw him, the centre of great meetings. 'When they applaud you, remember your failures,' said an old friend. After an amazing furlough he returned to China and wrote to his nephew Joseph Kimber Hill, who was at Richmond college preparing to join his uncle. He was having a good time at his weekend appointments, and was seeing conversions. 'The pulpit is a perilous place,' his uncle wrote. 'Keep low before the Lord; Joe, keep low before the Lord.' That saintly minister knew how little praise it took to turn a good man's head."

David Hill was a rich man's son from Yorkshire, who spent thirty-two years in central China, spending all his fortune not on himself but on others. Mr. Rattenbury as a young man tended the graves of missionaries in Hankow, including David Hill's. On his was inscribed in Chinese: 'The Son of Man came not to be ministered unto but to minister'. Across the tomb they wrote one word: 'Servant'.

"As latterly" went on the president, "I have read through the diaries, the notebooks, the pamphlets, the letters of David Hill, he has searched my soul. Some of us here were led to China through reading his life. He won more men and women to service overseas than any minister of whom I have heard. I never knew him till I saw him in those last private notes, that he would doubtless have destroyed had he known his last fatal illness was upon him.

"In some poor Chinese house you will find him, like the Chinese, up before dawn, to search his Greek Testament and pray. That Testament was his delight . . . Then through his tireless day of service for the poor, the sick in body or in soul, and back at night to review it all before his father and his God. They sometimes found him asleep upon his knees and left him there; for God would understand."

The ex-China missionary concluded his address by saying that the first text David Hill ever preached on, in Hankow, and the last he used in Britain thirty years later, was: "I beseech you therefore brethren, by the mercies of God, that you present your bodies a living sacrifice, holy, acceptable unto God, which is your reasonable service."

The Red Armies in China, while the Conference sat, were making considerable advances, and it was fitting that a devotional hour was given to a question and answer session on Christianity and Communism between Dr. W. E. Sangster and the Rev. Edward Rogers.

"The best way of thinking of Communism was by thinking of the three 'p's'," said Mr. Rogers, who was quoted by the *Methodist Recorder*. "Communism was a protest, a promise and a philosophy. The real root of Communism for many who had given their lives in its service was the protest against appalling exploitation and injustice. They had seen man's inhumanity to man, and had known life twisted, distorted and spoiled, and they felt life could be good and beautiful and they had risen. And they were inspired by the promise of Communism that a day would come when all would dwell in freedom and equity, and each would receive according to his need... The vigour of the methods of the Communists drew their reluctant admiration, but the methods themselves they could never accept."

Dr. Sangster asked Mr. Rogers what answer a Communist would give to the Psalmist's question: "What is man?"

"That is a question that the Communist doesn't like, because it reveals the fundamental confusion of his policy," said Mr. Rogers. "The Communist answer is that man is a part of nature — a material being who must work out his destiny in this life and world. Yet at the same time, by an unexplained jump in logic, man stands outside nature as an agent who directs and controls it. The two things do not go together. The only real answer to the question was given by the writer to the Hebrews. The answer to the question was shown to us in Jesus."

No one in the Conference, not even Stephen, guessed the complete victory Communism was about to achieve in China. The ex-President said that they remembered Chinese brethren with affection, and never more than in this time of confusion and disturbance, when the work in China was uncertain. But he had a note of optimism. "We believe the work you did will grow, even though it passes through days of tribulation. We shall remember that Church in our thoughts and prayers."

Stephen spoke at a Conference Welcome to Missionaries meeting in Chester and there was a ring of hope in his address. He told of China's travail under four periods of persecution and revolution: the Boxer uprising, the Anti-Christian movement instigated by students of Peking university; the Japanese occupation, and finally the threat of Communism. He believed that the present opposition would result in greater interest in Christian teaching and in new opportunities.

It was Mr. Rattenbury who was most anxious. At the Conference Overseas Missionary meeting he suddenly declared: "I have a feeling sitting here tonight that there is no sense of urgency even in this meeting, that it hasn't touched your hearts so that you feel you cannot go home and sleep because of it . . . We at the Mission House are disturbed because the signs of urgency have passed away, the urgency for people to give money, people to work, people to pray."

There is no evidence that even Stephen was aware of the urgency, but he was aware that in the streets of Liverpool there were many Chinese people who had made their home in the large northern port. On the streets, between sessions, he stopped and talked to them. Inevitably, when he explained why he was in Liverpool, the conversation swung round to Christianity.

"Have you ever heard of Jesus?" he asked.

"Who is that?"

"Have you ever been invited to attend a Christian church?"

"No."

"No one in this city has ever asked you to the Methodist Central Hall?"

He sought out Mr. Rattenbury in distress.

"Why do you send missionaries to China when there are Chinese in Liverpool for whom no Church is caring?" he asked abruptly.

There was an embarrassed silence.

"You had better look into the situation," the President suggested. "Stephen, you were right to speak to me of this."

He went back on to the streets, and into the poor section of the city where most of them lived in this bustling port on the Mersey.

In 1200 it was a fishing village, but it expanded in the seventeenth and early eighteenth centuries, through trading with the West Indies and the slave trade. In the 1840s the Irish potato famine had resulted in a big influx of Irishmen, but the Chinese were more recent.

"How long have you been in England?" he asked.

"Ten years . . . fourteen . . . twenty-three."

"And no minister or vicar has called on you?"

He was astounded, but a seed had been sown in his heart and mind.

Instinctively, he turned to the Methodist Church, button-holing officials in Liverpool, and asking that provision might be made for the spiritual needs of these people. All were sympathetic, but he was told to approach the Methodist Missionary Society. It was put on their agenda for discussion.

After a holiday Stephen went to spend a year at the Selly Oak Colleges in Birmingham, where he had been awarded the William Paton Lectureship, teaching students from ten countries about comparative religions and Chinese history.

He was in his element. He liked young people and the hours in the lecture-room were instructive for them and for him. A few planned to go to China, where in the first term the door for missionaries was partially open, but he underlined that they must have a knowledge of Chinese religions and customs to present the Gospel effectively.

"Christ was born in the Middle East, where East and West touched one another. Christianity spread in both directions," he said, "but while it triumphed in the West it made less impact in the East. The outcome is that Christ has been interpreted by Western minds, but Christ's teaching was for the whole world."

His lectures were sprinkled with anecdotes from everyday life in China.

If you go to a Chinese home where there is a funeral you will notice that the representatives of the three main religions are taking part. First you will see the Buddhist monks reading the Buddhist canons at one side of the dead person, while Taoist

priests read Taoists canons on the other side. There you will
also find a Confucian scholar to perform a solemn ceremony to
promote the dead person to be among his ancestors in order to
be able to accept offerings and sacrifice from the family members and relations. Though all religions are there, yet there is
no conflict. A Confucian holds the teaching of Confucius and at
the same time believes in Buddhism and Taoism.

In imagination he took them into Chinese homes to see Chinese
art.

As soon as you get into the sitting room, you will notice that it
is decorated with Chinese paintings and written pictures. They
are poems of lovely thought perpetuated in beautiful handwriting and hung upon the walls to suggest a mental picture. With
a written picture three things are necessary: the writing must
be beautiful: the writer must be a good man or a famous one:
the writing must be a poem or express some ethical or philosophical idea, or suggest a mental picture of landscape or social
condition. The writing itself to the Chinese eyes is a fine piece
of art. The Chinese scholars take years to practice how to write,
but with a brush and ink on a sheet of paper; few have
succeeded in reaching the standard achieved by ancient people.

He quizzed the students, and they questioned him, on what
Christianity had to offer that Buddhism did not supply? But if
they were to understand the religions of China they must also
know some of its history and so week by week he took them on a
journey through Chinese civilisation. He was able to explain the
Chinese mentality, so different from the Westerners, a point
young missionaries did not always grasp.

"The Chinese never want to conquer nature," he said. "If
there is a mountain in the way, the Chinese do not make a tunnel
through it, but change the desire of going forward. It is not a
disappointment, it is a psychological adaptation to environment.
This change of idea makes the Chinese quite happy. So there is a
common saying 'to feel satisfied with any circumstance'. If a

tragedy or a great loss happens to a Chinese, he will be satisfied with his misfortune by repeating some such proverbs as 'how do you know that this misfortune will not turn into good fortune?'

"If any natural calamity happens," he told the students, "you Westerners would approach it in a scientific way, finding the cause and working out a remedy. The Chinese, on the other hand, approach it in a mythical and philosophical way. They would interpret the cause of this natural calamity as due to disharmony between nature and man — man has done something wrong therefore nature has responded with this natural calamity to man's evil. Harmony with nature is the heritage of Chinese civilisation. Harmony with nature was the philosophy of the early sages."

But while he lectured immense changes were taking place in China; a revolution such as China had never known was uprooting the ideas and ways of centuries, and China was about to take the first steps towards being an industrial as well as political power.

The news was disturbing to those concerned with Christian mission. The Communists were triumphantly sweeping south, taking over schools and hospitals and all administration. City after city was being occupied until on October 1, 1949, Mao became Chairman of the People's Republic of China.

'Go forward, make mistakes, correct the mistakes, and go forward again.' The slogan was repeated, but the mistakes, including executions, could not always be corrected. Missionaries were being given small pieces of rice paper on which were printed the words: 'I wish to leave China of my own free will.' They were compelled to sign.

"Your government sent you to work here, so you could spy," they were told.

"God sent us," they replied. "The government knew nothing about it."

But the soldiers did not believe in God.

"Our Church made it possible for us to come," the missionaries went on to explain.

"How many people has your Church? We know you are telling lies. Your government sent you."

In some inland areas mission staff had to report daily to the Communist control office. If they failed to arrive soldiers fetched them and marched them through the town with machine-guns in their backs.

Stephen's wife expected him to be able to return as headmaster at Tangshan. She loved China and with her children waited for his return.

Each letter that arrived at Selly Oak from her made Stephen realise that he must not delay his return. If the missionaries had to leave his presence was more vital. He sat down and wrote a lengthy letter to the Methodist Missionary Society in London, and without delay they booked his return passage through Thomas Cook and Son. The students at Selly Oak gave him a good send-off and he travelled to London, to spend his last two or three days in England at a guest-house known as the House of Rest.

He had several visitors, among them Sister Gladys Stephenson, a Methodist missionary just back from China, after a lifetime's service. He questioned her closely, a little alarmed at the picture she painted. He had known of her sterling work as a hospital matron at Hankow, how she had been a pioneer in the training of Chinese nurses, and one-time President of the Nurses Association of China. For three years she was in a Japanese prison-camp. For a long time she had been the Rev. Rattenbury's next-door neighbour, and Stephen found himself completely at ease chatting with her, although he found that chatting consisted mostly of listening.

She was the kind of indefatigable professional which China needed in thousands, but because she was a missionary her services had been terminated and she had been compelled 'to leave China of her own free will'.

Stephen was dismayed, but saw it as a call to nationals like himself to play an increasing role, but it was not to be, for just before his departure a further letter came. His eyes ran down the page with utter horror. It could not be true.

The documentation for his return to Tangshan was on the desk in front of him, but the letter clearly said that he must not return.

He could not believe it. More carefully he read the letter a second time. There was no question about it. His school had been seized. He was headmaster no longer. His responsibility was over. He would almost certainly be arrested because of his close association with the West. He must not go back.

His heartbeat hammered into every line. The world had become a madhouse, with high walls made up of ideologies shutting men in and shutting men out. The strain of separation had already been great, now it would continue indefinitely . . . He should never have left.

He fingered the air ticket, checking on the flight time, then pushed it away in despair. In this dilemma what was God trying to say to him?

"O God, heavenly father . . ." It was painful even to pray.

He did not take off his clothes that night.

Later, he went on a visit to the continent. There he spent five nights tossing on his bed, unable to sleep, facing a crisis in which he sought God, questioned God, and tried to turn his face from God. The crisis was concerned with his family, with his own future, and with his spiritual state.

Bernard of Clairvaux had over his door the words: 'Bernard, why are you here?' Whenever he went into his room the challenge faced him. When Stephen saw a fellow-Chinese in Europe the question forced itself: 'Stephen, why are you here? Why has God not allowed you to return home?'

In the face of this challenge he came to the frightening conclusion that although he could lecture, write a thesis, and administrate, that although he was a successful educationalist, he could not now speak of his faith because of a lack of assurance.

He would have valued an hour with Wang Ming-tao, but in those night hours there was no one to whom he could turn. The Holy Spirit brought to his mind the experience of John Wesley.

Stephen, like Wesley in his early years, had never preached 'salvation by faith alone'. He now had the doubts which Wesley experienced in the weeks preceding the society meeting in Aldersgate. Wesley wrote in his *Journal* on April 22, 1738: "I could not comprehend of an *instantaneous work*. I could not understand how this faith should be given in a moment: how a man could *at once* be thus turned from darkness to light, from sin and misery to righteousness and joy in the Holy Ghost." On Sunday April 23, Wesley was confronted with four living witnesses who told "how the Saviour so quickly and so mightily has mercy on sinners and accepts them. They related one after the other how it had gone with them . . . John Wesley and the rest who were with him were as though struck dumb at these narratives," history records. Later, through the witness of those four Moravians he cried out, "Lord, help thou my unbelief!"

In those five sleepless nights God did an instantaneous work in the life of Stephen. There is a sense in which he died, died to himself, died to selfish ambition, and gave himself unreservedly to Christ.

For always he would look back to those nights as Wesley did to Aldersgate Street.

"I will no longer cheat God. He will have all there is of Stephen Wang."

The Holy Spirit [he afterwards wrote], guided me to the potter's house for a period of time, where he convinced me of the richness of our heavenly father, reminded me of how the early disciples left all behind, and revealed to me the message to preach "Jesus Christ, and him crucified", from whom we receive our wonderful salvation, that we sinners can become saints and the children of God. There I surrendered myself and offered myself as a piece of clay into God's hand to be moulded according to his wish. It was a glorious emancipation from old bondage and responsibilities, and a wonderful joy in a new career as an ambassador of Christ.

6

Wholehearted Love

"STEPHEN, at least for the present, you must forget about returning to China," informed missionary friends told him.

"The pain in my heart," he wrote to one, "is increasing so heavily that I feel it is nearly beyond my power to bear."

An expelled missionary from China spent a whole day with him explaining the new situation. He confirmed that his school had been taken over, and that there was no job available there for him. At best he would have to apply to the government for employment, and undergo six months' political training: if he was not received favourably he would face a political trial. A business which he had started with a few friends had been declared bankrupt in the spring, but he learned that his wife and children were in good health. His second daughter, Sung Ling, had offered herself to Christ for evangelistic work.

"I am very homesick," he confessed. "I hope that it will be possible for me to go back."

They discussed the alternatives. If his wife and family could leave China he might take an academic position in England or America, the missionary suggested. In both countries there were opportunities for qualified men. There would be security.

"Do not tempt me," Stephen said. "Until I can return to China I believe that God is calling me to work among the Chinese in Europe. I have been thinking very seriously of giving the rest of my life for the ministry."

A few weeks later he wrote to a former student at Selly Oak, now in Norway.

I have not yet made up my mind when I shall return to China. I must take some time to prepare myself initially for this decision. Meanwhile, I'm challenging the missionary societies to do some work among the Chinese in London and Liverpool, about two thousand in number. I spent half a day yesterday speaking to the China Inland Mission about this matter. I told them that I feel very grateful to you for sending missionaries to China, but I'm very sorry that so many Chinese on your doorstep have been entirely neglected spiritually. No one has ever done any work among them. Since you cannot send missionaries over to China why don't you appoint somebody to preach the Gospel to the Chinese in England?

They were greatly moved and they have expressed to plan for work like this in the near future. I will go to other places to make the same propaganda and hope the preaching among the Chinese in England will soon be started. If I become a preacher how do you think about it?

"Stephen Wang," a Methodist minister wrote, "has character, judgment, high intelligence, and the ability to make decisions. He is also very ambitious."

For fifty years he had been pulling himself upwards. Since his spiritual crisis he had stopped. He was no longer looking towards the top, but in the direction where he believed the finger of God was pointing. He had turned his back on the possibility of an academic position in America in favour of his own people in Europe. If he could not return to China soon maybe his wife and five children could come to England. He missed them all, but talked most of his youngest boy, and his daughter Sung Ling who had been his inspiration.

In October 1950, he wrote home four times and cabled once, but received no reply. To his correspondent in Norway he wrote:

I have many things to tell you, but I cannot do so now. I had better tell you one thing which is important. Through these days of struggle, I have come nearer and nearer to the Lord. I feel to preach to the Chinese is my duty. Yesterday I came from Liverpool where I visited our Chinese people and distributed to them about one hundred Chinese Gospels and pamphlets. Last evening I attended the Westminster Central Hall autumn conference. There were more than three thousand people to listen to the report on China and to see the film about China, but the film was out of date because China has changed.

By November 1950, the decision had been finalised in his mind. "I am now," he wrote, "an evangelist among the Chinese in London and Liverpool. There is a lot of work to do. I have no connection with any missionary society but an independent movement. This is the way to make a good use of the rest of my life to win souls for the Lord."

"You will find me not a teacher but an evangelist," he wrote in December, enclosing a copy of George Dempster's book *Lovest Thou Me*, with encouragement to read the first chapter carefully because it gave a general idea of the dark influence in London's east end, where he was working.

The Methodist Missionary Society although not sponsoring his ministry was to make him a small personal allowance, and the *Methodist Recorder* asked their correspondent to interview him.

"You know the east end of London?" he asked the correspondent. "You know Chinatown. There are many more of my people living in London than you might perhaps believe. The same is true of Liverpool, of Cardiff, and to some degree of other cities. Then there are the men who come ashore from ships in the docks. They come and go without any to make friends with them. There is no place where they can find friendship among their own people.

"That is also true of those who live here. Most of them have to struggle to make a living. They are often employed in restaurants and laundries where their wages are low and, becoming gripped by their own material needs, they adopt a materialistic outlook and any thought of the spiritual life is crowded out."

The Methodist Missionary Society, overtaxed by changing world conditions created by the war, did not feel itself in a position to pursue further a missionfield at home but several of its members took a detailed interest in Stephen's activities.

Scores of missionaries from various societies were returning from China to England and he looked to them to support an interdenominational work, founded on prayer and maintained by faith. A prayer group was formed in Liverpool, and on December 31, 1950, at the end of the day, he wrote telling a friend how he and ten others had gathered in London 'to pray for spiritual revival among ourselves and among the Churches in different lands'.

On Sunday January 7, 1951, the Chinese Church in London was born in the home of Mr. and Mrs. K. T. Fan. Mr. Fan was working in the School of Oriental and African Studies. There were thirteen at the service, including nine Chinese. In a few months the Fans' home proved too small for the services, and they were transferred to London's Central Y.M.C.A. At the first anniversary service, on January 6, 1952, one hundred and thirty people were present.

Stephen was introduced to the Rev. Fred Harding of St. Albans, a banker in the City of London, as a result of an encounter at the British and Foreign Bible Society triple-jubilee conference at Swanwick. Miss Lily Armitt, who had taught Stephen as a boy when she was a missionary in China, attended the conference. There she met Fred Harding whom she had also known since he was a boy in London's east end. As Mr. Harding was registering at the conference he came face to face with Sister Lily, as he affectionately knew her. Within a short time she was telling him of Stephen's vision for the Chinese in Europe.

"Fred, would you consider advising him and being his treasurer?" she asked.

He was not looking for extra responsibilities, but agreed that Sister Lily might arrange a meeting. It took place on the steps of St. Paul's Cathedral. In the shadow of Sir Christopher Wren's masterpiece many historic momentous events had taken place, but Stephen was occupied with the present day.

"When I arrived at St. Paul's," Fred Harding recalls, "he was waiting for me. He was more obvious to me than I was to him, of course. I saw a tall, modestly well-built man in early middle life. Introductions were made and common friends mentioned. I was impressed with his quiet dignity, gracious manner and his obvious respectful attention to what I had to say. At once he plunged into an account of his experiences and hopes for the future. I was further impressed by his enthusiasm. This first meeting was succeeded by scores of others when we lunched together."

When Sister Lily had advised Stephen of his need for a treasurer, he had replied that without money a treasurer was useless, but he was for ever thankful for the introduction to Fred Harding and for the years in which he stood by him. Shortly before they met Mr. Harding had been called as lay pastor to the Independent Chapel in St. Albans, an old foundation of the Congregational Union, and Stephen was frequently to be the preacher.

Soon Stephen was being a guest in various Chinese homes. The introduction was often made when he gave someone in the street a booklet or a few passages from the Gospels in Chinese. When they could read, the Chinese always loved to find something in their own language, and it was an easy way to give them an approach to the Christian faith.

Although his ministry prospered, a cloud lingered. Letters from China were not reassuring. The hope of reunion was to be with him for years, but a kind Heavenly Father was shielding him from a complete knowledge of the future. There were periods of anguish lasting many weeks. He tried to picture his family growing up. It was easier with the older children, but he found it difficult with the youngest boy.

In 1951 news came from China that every Methodist had been told by the Communists to sign a Patriotic Covenant. The English translation of this document which follows is from the recently published *Religious Policy and Practice in Communist China* edited by Donald MacInnis, recommended to all serious students of China.

Chinese Christian Methodist Church Patriotic Covenant
1. We sincerely support Chairman Mao, the Chinese

Communist Party, the People's Government, the Common Platform, and all the laws and actions of the People's Government.

2. We will unite all Christians in supporting world peace, and in opposing American imperialist re-arming of Japan, and will take part in the movement to oppose America, aid Korea, and protect our homes and our country.

3. We will promote the Reform Movement in the Christian Church, complete the work of Self-government, Self-support, and Self-propagation, and so help the work of religion among the Chinese people, so as to serve them.

4. We will help the People's Government to get rid of spies and special agents, and be on the alert to prevent reactionary elements from using the Church in their destructive activities. We will clear the Church of all renegades, so as to preserve the purity of religion.

5. We will forever cut off all relations with American imperialism, and will completely wipe out of our Church all the influences of American cultural imperialism.

6. We will increase our study of current events, and our understanding of the government. We will take part in the labour movement, practise simple living, and strengthen the unity of the Chinese people.

> Each person accepting the Covenant should sign here.

Some Methodists refused to sign.

Stephen preserved, often re-reading, the letters from his daughter, Sung Ling, written between November 1948 and May 1950. At first she was an undergraduate at Yenching university, studying education, sharing in the upheaval as both lecturers and students left Peking to move south away from the advancing Red Army. She noted that the missionary professors were less inclined to run away, but knew that soon the Chinese would have to take over all academic responsibility. There was a temporary lull, and she used it to start a Sunday school class near the university, in a rented room. In the autumn term other students commenced

Sunday schools in the countryside, but by November were being hampered by heavy snow which blocked roads outside the city.

After graduating Sung Ling became a youth worker in a Peking church, her salary being 300 lb. of millet, but in prayer she believed God revealed to her that she must not accept such payment but live by faith.

I want to share with you a little more about myself so that you can pray for me [she wrote to her father]. Also I seek to know your view. As I look ahead to the future in China I believe God will raise up young people who like the Apostles will sacrifice all for the Gospel. They will not be afraid to suffer, to be poor and hungry, and even to die. After much prayer I have accepted this challenge and I have told the Church that I do not wish to be paid a salary. Such a request was new to them and had to be carefully considered, but I insisted they accepted. For all my need I look to God.

After one year I have experienced the real blessing behind faith. Formerly I heard of God but now I have experienced his provision. This testimony has challenged the Church and presented a living witness before the young people. They have kindly asked me to continue the work in autumn 1950, but I am seeking God's will without which all is in vain.

Although her faith was robust Stephen was concerned that physically she was overtaxing herself. He wrote about this, and her reply did not settle his mind.

"My health has not been good," she confessed. "My stomach has troubled me for months. God knows I need rest not only in body but in soul."

She found refreshment that summer in a conference sponsored by Wang Ming-tao, which was addressed by Dr. Chia Yu Ming. Although still in her early twenties such was her maturity that she was made responsible for the devotional sessions at the conference. There was an urgency infused in every prayer and talk. Apart from God's grace the future appeared unendurable.

Stephen found solace in what was being accomplished through

her, but there was other news which gave him hours of misery and numbness. Again he thanked God for his wife, who was carrying gigantic responsibilities.

"No matter what happens," wrote Sung Ling, "I believe she will remain faithful to God. She has great plans and hopes for all her children, but because of the complete change in our society all her hopes will not be fulfilled. What we need is not more food or clothing, but a real spiritual hunger."

Mother, acting prudently, had questioned her daughter's desire to give herself to Christian work. In a Communist society she also knew the danger. Sung Ling saw herself in the midst of a battlefield.

Mother wants me to be of more use in society, have a better position and status, but I believe God has heard my prayer and made her think differently. Maybe one day like Paul I will make tents to support myself. More and more I feel we as a family have been favoured by God, and that if we leave him now he will chastise us because of love. Our home, our country, need your prayer. There are many things that would comfort you.

She did not fully understand that she and her father, although separated by thousands of miles, were taking the same irrevocable steps. For both the natural wish, in view of their ability, was to seek security, position, comfort, but both saw God directing them to an uncharted way. They were being called away from the academic world, and they turned to the story of Abraham.

"By faith Abraham, when he was called, obeyed to go out into a place which he was to receive for an inheritance; and he went out, not knowing whither he went."

There is no call except to come out, [said the Chinese preacher, Watchman Nee]. Abraham was at home in the world with its established order, its advanced culture, its justifiable pride of attainment, and he was called to come out of that world to fulfil the purpose of God. That is the divine calling . . . Both the call of Abraham and the reason for his response lay in God. Once behold the God of glory and you must believe, you cannot do otherwise. Thus it was by faith — faith in the God of glory — that Abraham, when he was called, obeyed to go out.

Many university students were experiencing the divine calling. In Peking, Wang Ming-tao had seen his church attendance increase to more than a thousand, but as the building held only seven hundred the overflow sat in the courtyard. The growth was largely of students, teachers and government clerks. The emphasis in his preaching was on the existence of God and the power of the Spirit for Christian living. Throughout China belief in God was being ridiculed. Cynics were not saying God was dead, but that he had never existed except in the peasant mind. In all preaching it was necessary to go back to the starting point of the Christian creed: "I believe in God, the Father Almighty, Maker of Heaven and Earth."

In the universities there was a jump in the numbers seeking baptism and Wang Ming-tao's magazine *Spiritual Food* was increasing in circulation among undergraduates. Copies were passed from one to another, and only put aside when they were in tatters. Passages like 'He that loseth his life shall find it . . .' were heavily underlined.

In many villages and smaller towns in inland China worship was banned, Bibles confiscated, and church buildings used for other purposes, but in major cities there was greater freedom, and denominational churches, under supervision, were continuing limited programmes. Revival and evangelistic services were often impossible, but even where public worship had ceased there were meetings in family groups.

Though the government says its policy is freedom of religion [wrote Sung Ling], some of its officers act rather differently. The government when challenged admits that some officers have been extreme and promises to correct them, but their main aim is to cut off completely all financial support from Western missions. No extension of the Church is allowed.

Churches already closed must not reopen, and no new churches are allowed. We must rethink what is the best way to preach the Gospel. Our quality of life, and our prayer, is so important. I believe the latter glory will be greater than the former.

She told him of the rapid growth of the independent Churches known as the Little Flock. They were a disciplined community, the members showing great love for each other. If a member missed a communion service he was visited to find out why. Members of the denominational Churches like herself, who wished to deepen their spiritual life were attending their devotional meetings. She found them a little exclusive, for their members did not participate in the activities of any other Church, and did not join in with the Christian unions in the university.

"Yet their love for God and for each other sets a wonderful example. Their absolute obedience to the elders and their loyalty to the work assigned to them is outstanding. In Shanghai quite a few have been sent to the south-west of China to give themselves for pioneer work in the Gospel."

Not quite so exclusive was the Rev. David Yang, former vice-principal of a Shanghai Bible seminary, later minister of a Nangking church. He was writing that China's need was to train thousands of lay-workers, spiritually-minded men and women, who were not necessarily academics, but who were willing to endure hardship and had a burden for pioneer ministry. They were needed to fill the gap left by the departing missionaries.

At the meeting in Yenching university Sung Ling responded, and was encouraged to go for a period of study to a Shanghai Bible seminary. It meant going far away from home and leaving the Church youth work in which she had established herself. The Church leaders urged her to stay for a further year, but she had compulsion to go to Shanghai, although she realised that being publicly associated with the Gospel would also mean sharing in the sufferings of Christ.

My desire is to be rooted in the Spirit, to be a worker without blame. I must leave behind the enjoyment of the privileged educated class and share in the suffering of the majority of Chinese. Only by sharing their way of life can we be qualified to give them the Gospel. Missions in the past have paid too much attention to their own standard of life. They have isolated themselves from the Chinese, living in ivory towers, using money to hire Chinese to do their work, while God's sheep are wandering between the mountains and the hills.

Very recently one missionary told me I must adopt their standard of living and not be the same as the Chinese. What a pity and God's work sadly unfinished. If we don't realise this crisis and the urgent need for workers how can there be any hope for the Chinese Church? All my fellow students live by faith. The seminary with its sixty students has no financial backing from denominations. I am learning with them. To trust God is the first lesson I must learn.

Mother did not say much about my coming to the seminary. Will you please pray for us all. Though some have fallen away God has not withdrawn his love; His rod and His staff are still with us.

She told her father how a party of students had been to visit the Jesus Home. Since Communist rule the Jesus Home had attracted much attention because it was indigenous, and very practical in life and faith. Surprisingly, it had received some nods of approval from the new government, not because of its spirituality, but because of its freedom from Western influence.

A tutor in the school of religion at Yenching had accompanied the students and afterwards had written an article for the university bulletin. Stephen had a copy of this, and found it so impressive that he had it translated and typed for private circulation. It was introduced by the bulletin editor who said that to a certain group of people religion was only a ritual garment, an off-duty enjoyment, like music or art. To others it was a refuge in time of danger; to some an insurance for life after death; to others a theological argument; to still more merely an expression of loyalty in propagating and defending denominationalism. But to the Jesus Home religion was the whole life.

It was founded by Mr. Ching Tien-ying, and there were nearly two hundred organised communities throughout China. Several students from Yenching had joined him over the years. All members lived together, cultivated spiritual life and worshipped together.

"They also endeavour to produce and serve by both division of labour and by co-operation, in order to form a Christian community of love to achieve communistic and productive construction."

The writer visited five Jesus Homes in various provinces, including the first and largest in Shantung. Stephen prepared a summary of the tutor's impressions.

Since the establishment of the first Home, more than twenty years have elapsed. After having seen the Home with our own eyes we realise that the Home possesses a power of inspiration certainly beyond the reach of any ordinary church. According to my judgment and analysis its basic dynamic power, in spite of its varied expressions, is the love of Jesus Christ. The love of God revealed in Jesus Christ through his suffering and death on the cross for sinners has attracted them, inspired them, and controlled them to such an extent that they have offered before the cross their complete surrender, complete obedience, and complete consecration. Therefore they are able to gain the victory of life in the following ways.

1. Complete self-denial by the abandoning of their earthly possessions, the leaving of all behind, and the taking up of their cross. The founder of the Jesus Home and others established the Home by giving all their property to it. Now, anyone who joins gives all his property.

2. Wholehearted love of the Lord, and denial of the world, that is to say they discard 'the lusts of the flesh, the lust of the eyes, and the vainglory of life', in order to love the Lord, serve the Lord, and to bear witness. Mr. Ching regards

wealth, lust and vainglory as the hindrances that prevent
Christian believers from loving the Lord.

3. Wholehearted love of men.

People in the Jesus Home fast on Sunday mornings, and
the cost of breakfast is earmarked as an offertory. They also
go out in groups to work for others without pay. Thus it
seems they absolutely follow the teachings of Jesus and St.
Paul, forgetting themselves in thinking of others. To those
who ask for medical help they give it impartially. They have
a small out-patient clinic and hospital accommodation.

When Stephen circulated the article he said that it seemed to
him that it was written without the slightest desire to do any
propaganda for the Jesus Homes, but was a sincere statement of
personal impressions. He was convinced of the significant part the
Jesus Home had played and was playing, together with other
indigenous Churches, to spread the Gospel in China.

7

The Exodus

IN LONDON Stephen was supported by some C.I.M. missionaries on furlough, and the unique 'little pint-sized missionary lady' Gladys Aylward, who did deputation work. Gladys Aylward had not yet achieved international fame through the book *The Small Woman* by Alan Burgess. She was barely five feet in height and from being a parlourmaid in London had served for twenty years as a missionary in China becoming a legendary figure. She loved the Chinese wherever they were. A strong individualist whatever time she was allocated as a speaker she rarely took less than one hour, but for most of those who listened even this was not sufficient.

It is doubtful if she would have ever returned to England if the Japanese had not beaten her, inflicting severe internal injuries. The doctors she consulted insisted that she returned to England for an operation, but she had no money for the fare, no society sponsoring her. American generosity came to her aid and she finally sailed for England which she had not seen for twenty years.

And then she was home-sick for China.

In the Chinese Church she found solace.

"Use me, God," she prayed, exactly as she had twenty-five years before when she was certain in her mind that her life-work was to be a missionary in China. For a while her name found its way on to the notepaper of the Chinese Church, but the link was never clearly defined, and it was better that way, although a sympathetic understanding existed between her and Stephen which was a strength to both. She was a naturalised Chinese, and they had both experienced hardship during the Japanese occupation. While he had led a party to safety through the Japanese lines, she had taken one hundred Chinese children on a twelve-day march over the mountains to the Yellow River.

After she had appeared on the B.B.C. television programme *This is Your Life* she received an invitation to tea with the Queen of England at Buckingham Palace.

When Stephen heard that she planned to arrive at the Palace in a London taxi, he arranged for a prosperous member of his Church to chauffeur her in his impressive car. Afterwards Stephen took her to the House of Commons and the House of Lords, but it was a hasty visit for she was anxious to return to her basement flat in Marble Arch where she was more relaxed.

"To Gladys," Burgess wrote, "her God was a suit of chain-mail, proof against any arrow or bullet the mortal world could fire at her. Her faith was durable; it was like a warm blanket on a cold night, medicine when she was sick, food on the table, a roof over her head, a bed in which she could lie enfolded and secure. None of the intellectual problems of the theologians ever troubled her; the fears and dilemmas of the doubting intellectuals blew above her head at stratospheric level."

Stephen who had moved among intellectuals for thirty years found her faith infectious, and she moved with ease among the Chinese he gathered together, no task being too humble, no opportunity too great. With the publication of *The Small Woman* she became so much in demand as a speaker that he saw less of her than he wished.

The Chinese Church was steadily growing. Holiday conferences were held in resorts like Frinton-on-Sea and Eastbourne, and Stephen made time to visit Liverpool eighteen times during 1951 and 1952, calling on Chinese laundries, seamen's restaurants and knocking on doors.

Sister Lily Armitt who had introduced him to Fred Harding proved an ally. When she taught him as a boy, because of her fair hair and blue eyes, he thought of her as an angel. When he was headmaster she taught music at Tangshan school. Now retired, her home was in Mansfield, more than one hundred miles from London, but Stephen travelled there to discuss his problems, finding warmth in the home she shared with a friend.

In the early fifties food rationing continued in England, and the two women saved their eggs and bacon, which he relished, when a visit was near. After the meal Sister Lily would object, but was unable to stop the former headmaster from washing the dishes, vacuuming the carpet, and fetching in the coal, while she sewed on his buttons and darned his socks.

When he first visited the Mansfield home Sister Lily told her friend that they must not call him by his Christian name. In China, she explained, only his wife called him Stephen, but she found he was no longer the slightly austere figure she remembered; he had changed, and soon they were calling him Stephen.

The Church in London proved to be a base for wider developments. Chinese services were commenced at the Malayan Teachers' College, Wolverhampton; and teams visited Cardiff, Scotland, Rotterdam, Brussels, Paris and West Germany.

In the home of Mr. Harding at St. Albans the Chinese Overseas Christian Mission was inaugurated.

"The chief aim of the Mission," Stephen declared, "is to carry a positive evangelism to the Chinese outside China, and to bring them a knowledge of the full Gospel of salvation through our Lord Jesus Christ. The work is based upon the simple preaching of the Bible as the inspired Word of God. It is desired to help the Chinese Christians to establish their own Church in accordance with the principle of self-support, self-management and self-government."

The direction of the C.O.C.M. was discussed at length with Fred Harding over lunch. They visualised a militant body of evangelists rather than an institution; having activity among people, rather than being housed in large and expensive buildings. They looked forward to seeing a multiplicity of groups of Chinese Christians in many places — towns, colleges, hospitals — made up of restaurant workers, students and nurses, together with the families of permanent residents. They hoped that the Churches would take local Chinese groups under their wing and assist them.

Soon some churches were allowing such groups to meet on their premises to the advantage of the Chinese and the local members.

Bishop Frank Houghton was the first chairman of the Chinese Overseas Christian Mission. He had sailed for China in 1920, and was consecrated Bishop of Szechwan, in 1937. From 1940 until 1951 he was the General Director of the China Inland Mission. He was the author of many hymns including a favourite of Stephen's:

> Facing a task unfinished,
>   That drives us to our knees,
> A need that, undiminished,
>   Rebukes our slothful ease;
> We, who rejoice to know Thee,
>   Renew before Thy throne
> The solemn pledge we owe Thee
> To go and make Thee known.

At the beginning of this century a C.I.M. leader was able to write: "The blessing is coming. China is being opened up. The last provincial capital has flung wide its gates — the messenger of the Gospel has entered in. Today, any city in China may be entered without let or hindrance. The walls of conservatism are tottering to their fall; the barriers of seclusion are broken down. China yields at last — the Rock has opened!"

Fifty years later China was closed. The day of opportunity had passed. Chinese Christians were urged to remove imperialistic elements from within the Church, to march under the flag of opposition to imperialism, under the direction of the People's Government to build a new China.

Church members were instructed to wipe out the 'fear America, worship America, fawn on America' thinking, and to learn to hate, despise, and vilify American imperialism. While any support was received from overseas it was stated that the Churches would be used to carry out aggression against China. The Protestant Churches were brought under the control of the Religious Affairs Bureau of the Central government, which became known as the Three Self Movement; self-support, self-government and self-propagation.

Chou En-lai told Chinese Christians: "So we are going to go on letting you teach, trying to convert people . . . After all we both believe that truth will prevail; we think your beliefs are untrue and false, therefore if we are right, the people will reject them, and your Church will decay. If you are right, then the people will believe you, but we are prepared for that risk."

In newspaper articles, speeches and discussion groups religion was described as the opiate of the people. It made people pray for a good harvest instead of working; it made them look to gods instead of their own resources; it was harmful to physical and mental health, and to China's well-being. In the new nation there was no room for religious superstition; it belonged to a primitive society. Christianity was often linked with ancestor worship, witchcraft, spirit worship, Taoism and Buddhism, in the minds of the writers of these pieces.

Stephen sought out the returning missionaries to get the latest news. During 1951 among the hundreds who left China were six hundred from the C.I.M. Many were battered in spirit and jangled in nerves after the apparent catastrophe in China, and with little vision of the future. Gilbert Vinden asked:

Is the work finished? The answer must be *No* as long as there are millions who have never heard the Gospel. Is our work for the time being finished? The answer would seem to be *Yes*, since God in his wisdom is allowing a complete withdrawal of missionary aid, in order that the Chinese Church may realise its independence, or rather, to spell the word in another way, its god-dependence. We leave with real pain and regret, and yet with the realisation that our leaving is of the Lord, and with strong hope that, with all mission crutches taken away, the Church in many places will walk on in a spirit of God-reliance.

When the missionaries left there was often desolation. Stephen shared the anguish in the letters from China which found their way to the House of Rest where he was living. Sometimes he shared them with other residents, sometimes they were too private, and he destroyed them. Carrying essentials, in an atmosphere of defeat, the missionaries said their sad farewells, leaving behind words of encouragement, as they walked out of buildings which they had helped erect, boarding ships and aircraft never to return. They left behind schools and hospitals and believers, amongst them his own family, and they hated to go.

A missionary went to say goodbye to a blind beggar woman to give her a small sum to help in the days ahead. The blind beggar refused, and on the day of the missionary's departure, although she was extremely poor, she pressed into the missionary's hand a small gift towards her travelling expenses, bravely saying, regardless of those around: "I have come to say goodbye to you, to you who have brought me out of darkness into light."

Some, having been told to quit, had to wait weeks or months for travel papers. The Deputy China director wrote: "The future of the C.I.M. is a secret which is hid in the heart of God. The things that are revealed belong to us but the secret things belong to the Lord our God."

About this time a best-selling book was published written by Han Suyin, a writer born in Peking. Entitled *A Many Splendoured Thing* it described the departure of the missionaries. It was recommended to Stephen. Although a novel he found much of it rang true. It described an evening in the Church Guest House in Hong Kong.

In this room were the people who had worn down our traditions, broken our selfishness, awakened our social conscience, armed us with ideals, dragged our scholars from their poetic torpor and our peasants' superfluous babies from the cesspits, built our universities, our hospitals, and our puritanism ... Although now we cast them out as instruments of foreign aggression, they had also made us. We were part of each other.

In the novel a missionary points out a fair young man with an English newspaper who has been fifty-nine days in prison, suspected of spying. The missionary talked of the seed of Christianity which had been planted on Chinese soil. Would it thrive without subsidy or dependence? This was the test.

"We had become too smug," the missionary confessed, "too comfortable, with our servants and our furloughs, our missionary compounds away from the Chinese people. We dabbled in power, especially us Methodists, we had so much influence with the last government . . . The Chinese Church must now carry on Christianity. I have faith in God and in your people."

Stephen was not only able to listen to the returning missionaries, but was able to discuss intelligently with them the future. Sadly, he confessed, whatever the coming years might hold for the Chinese Church in China, there was no part in it for missionaries. So far as his country was concerned they were now out of a job, and must look elsewhere. Some took up teaching posts, or entered the home ministry, but soon 250 C.I.M. missionaries, for example, had returned for new tasks in east Asia. Entering new missionfields proved difficult.

Arnold J. Lea, the C.I.M. Overseas Director, wrote: "Possibly most frustrating of all is the Babel of languages encountered in most places. Imagine the feeling of impotency to find oneself, an old China hand, amongst a group of chatting Chinese in Malaya and not able to understand a single word, for though they are speaking their own language, they are conversing in another dialect from that known by the missionary."

Stephen was kept in touch with the situation in China by regular letters from Sung Ling. When possible he read extracts to the Chinese Church in London. They stimulated prayer, and demonstrated that the Holy Spirit was enabling men to speak God's message with boldness. They challenged those who listened.

On November 29, 1950, Sung Ling wrote:

I received your letter forwarded from Peking to Shanghai. To know you are well is a great comfort. It is two months since I arrived at the seminary in Shanghai. To leave my work in Peking has given me an opportunity for more rest and for time to be quiet before the Lord. My health has improved.

Although life in south China is different from the north adjustment has been easy because I have accepted this by the grace of God. We have sixty students from various backgrounds, and of different ages, but we all live happily and in his love. Our desire to be trained by him has drawn us together. It is difficult to buy Greek textbooks and lexicons, but fortunately we discovered about twelve books in one bookshop in Shanghai so we bought them all. I hoped to have a dictionary but it is impossible to buy one in China though I am told they are obtainable in England. The title is *The Analytical Greek Lexicon*, and I wonder if you could buy one for me, also a Greek Bible.

I heard from mother some days ago and she is well. She is not working but is looking after Hung (the youngest son, who was finishing his primary education). He has improved considerably in his school and acts quite maturely. How I hope that God may have his life. Gigi is still teaching in Union Medical College, Peking. Brother is busy as a doctor, but his health is poor.

Before the summer holiday I fractured my kneecap and you kindly wrote and asked about the operation. I expected to enter hospital at the end of July but there was no bed available. Doctors who were my college friends tried to assist, without success. In the middle of August there was the summer students Christian conference in Peking. I obtained permission to attend now hoping to go into hospital at the end of August. The main speaker was Dr. Chia. I was profoundly helped and the Lord stirred up revival. Among the leaders was Cheng, now a fellow student in the seminary. He spoke powerfully and exercised the gift of healing. The conference had a special day for healing, and those who had faith were asked to prepare themselves. On the day between four and five hundred went forward to be anointed with oil. The total attendance was more than one thousand.

I went forward and I was healed instantly. Before this my

knee was painful and I could neither ride a cycle nor walk much. When I went forward I was unable to kneel. I had been warned by many people that if I did not take care TB might develop in the joint. Now every day I climb up to the third floor more than ten times without difficulty. The conference lasted ten days and at the end I decided to come to this seminary to study. There is now no need for me to go into hospital.

Pray for the Church in China. The Churches in Peking remain the same as before. In the summer conference many young people from different colleges, universities and high schools were revived, and offered themselves to God with much courage. In these days God is greatly using Miss Sheng, the co-worker of Miss Bee, to continue the revival. The Christian Union attendance has increased from just over one hundred to more than three hundred. God is going to light the torch of revival especially using Miss Bee and Dr. Chai. Two weeks ago Miss Bee was speaking at revival meetings in the Baptist church which was so packed there was nowhere to put one's feet. Many repented and were filled with the Holy Spirit, and many were healed. At the end three hundred dedicated themselves waiting to be called into work for God. I believe the fire of revival will continue to burn in the big Churches which have slept for so long.

When you have time let me know about the condition of the Churches in England so that we in China can pray for them.

I pray that God's grace may follow you always and guide you to return to China soon. In our seminary the Greek lecturer has just returned from America. He's a former graduate who has spent some time studying theology there. Miss Lee had returned from Szechwan and remembers meeting you in 1944 when she was working with the Rev. David Yang. Many students here know of you which makes their fellowship in the Lord more precious to me. David Yang has received a special light and burden from God concerning the future strategy of the Church in China. The Little Flock remains exclusive with little fellowship with other Churches, but their own membership has increased rapidly. There has been some division in the Christian Unions because of this which is not glorifying to God.

She wrote again on December 17, 1950.

Since my arrival in Shanghai I have sent you two letters, but have you received them? I am anxious about your health and your work. As it is very near Christmas I am sure the English homes must be celebrating. Formerly in China even in non-Christian shops there were Christmas trees, but now of course this is impossible. The celebrations in churches continue. Two years ago we did not expect still to have this freedom which is a special blessing from God.

There is much anti-American feeling here about the Korean war, and numerous young people have offered themselves to be trained for military service. The condition of the Church is about the same. In the countryside the preaching of the Gospel becomes more difficult, and some places no longer allow Christians to meet, but in the large cities we still have freedom. My seminary is going on well, and we finish this term in the middle of January. I don't think I'll go home for the vacation, but will probably stay in the school. We have sixty students, it is very crowded and the waiting list is long. God has raised many university students to forsake all to follow him. This seems beyond human explanation but God has done it.

When I'm tired and busy my stomach gives me a little trouble, but it will be all right if I pay attention to my diet and rest. I find the Greek lessons become more difficult and are not as easy to remember, I must put more time into it for it is interesting. Our Greek lecturer who has returned from America lectures in English and I find it good to use my English.

Will you pray that I may love the Lord and serve Him? I know it will be your joy if I have a life and work which is pleasing to God. Since my arrival here my spiritual life has developed. Dr. Chia is a fine teacher and guide. His encouragement has benefited all of us, and we have learned much Biblical doctrine. Miss Bee has been a considerable help not only in our studies but also in revealing the deeper life of prayer. I heard from mother yesterday that everyone is well at home. The eldest brother was married on December 3. Write and let me know how you are when you have time. I pray and wish you well.

Then letters became irregular. From his window he watched the arrival of the postman, and hurried downstairs to look in vain for correspondence from China. After eight months without news he confided to a friend: "It is heart-breaking. Really I don't know how to manage this separation with dear ones for a time unknown. Well, his grace is sufficient. I have to learn how to be patient and to wait upon God."

At Whitsun, Stephen made a pilgrimage to Cliff College, Calver, in Derbyshire, which has been called 'the evangelical outpost of Methodism'. Some fifteen thousand were present for the Whit-Monday convention meeting. Dr. W. E. Sangster was a regular convention speaker, and Stephen shared his vision of the Church with every member a serious, devout and practising Christian.

"I have a vision of our public services so full of the power of the Holy Spirit that people coming in *casually* could feel the impact and be made 'convertible material' almost in the singing of a hymn. I have a vision of hundreds of souls reborn in God, and thousands going right on to a sanctified life," Dr. Sangster had said.

"I was greatly inspired at Cliff College," Stephen wrote when he returned to London, "and came to the conviction that without the Holy Spirit we can do nothing."

He often referred to Cliff. He had read of Samuel Chadwick, a former principal of the college, who had died on October 16, 1932, but whose influence lived on in Methodism and in wider circles through his books *The Path of Prayer* and *The Way to Pentecost*. Like Stephen, Samuel Chadwick had come from a poor home, starting work in a cotton mill when he was eight, but in later years he said God had brought him up among the under-privileged that in later life he might minister to them.

Some modern Methodists, Stephen found, talked little of conversion, but Chadwick used to tell of night calls 'to go and pray with souls in the anguish of hell'. He sent his students out from Cliff in the expectancy that they would be used of God in the conversion of people. A Pentecostal experience flooded the whole life of the college. Samuel Chadwick wrote:

The fire of Pentecost is a blaze of moral and spiritual enthusiasm. It is a passion for God that sets personality ablaze. Every part of the man is aflame. I can speak for myself. Pentecost came to me in my twenty-second year. I had been a Christian from boyhood; and a very serious and earnest Christian as best I knew, but Pentecost was a miracle of power. The fire of God quickened my mortal body, it vitalised every faculty, it gave me a new mentality, and opened to me a new world of spiritual reality. The fire kindled to a flame. So it is at Cliff. Every man is aflame for God.

"Let it constantly burn in my heart," Stephen prayed, "so that their motto is mine, 'Christ for All: All for Christ'."

How he wished there had been a Chinese Cliff College in Peking!

He attended the Keswick convention, and was able to meet a variety of Christian leaders and missionaries. He shared his burden for the Chinese in Europe and found sympathetic ears. He needed the memory of the tent meetings and the encouragement as he later tramped from home to home, sometimes for a whole day in the rain, in Liverpool or London.

He found the Chinese mostly in shabby streets, in decaying houses, living in isolation from their neighbours. After a visit to Liverpool he wrote:

It is an entirely different environment, very smoky and dirty in the centre of the city and near the docks.

There are thousands of seamen from various parts of the

world hunting for the opposite sex. In the evenings, there are hundreds of bad women and girls moving about on the corners of the main streets and walking in and out of cafés. It is a very serious social problem.

Our Chinese population, now about four thousand in number, are mostly engaged in restaurant, laundry and services on the boats. They are not educated and their way of life is not very satisfactory. To work among them is not an easy job. It is a great battle against social evil and ignorance. It needs greater sacrifice and more fighting spirit to do this work effectively. There is no one at present to take care of it. I must come at least once a month for a week or so.

When he needed a new pair of shoes he tried not to be disheartened that he could not afford them, thanking God that at least his feet were not shackled. When bills began to mount and his treasurer wrote to say there was only £2 in the bank he turned to his *Daily Light* to read: 'A just man falleth seven times and riseth up again.'

When funds were more plentiful he was able to visit Chinese families in Belgium, Denmark, France, Norway and Holland. In Copenhagen on one visit he called on five Chinese restaurants. In Amsterdam, Leiden and Delft he visited students.

Under the wonderful guidance of God [he wrote from Holland], I have met the Chinese Christians in an unexpected way, just like a miracle. It is now half past four in the morning. After breakfast I will visit a Chinese company selling textiles. Afterwards I will see three Chinese old people. In the evening I will have a meal in a Chinese Christian's home, meeting other Christians. On Tuesday I will visit students in Delft. On Wednesday I leave for Paris. A heavier programme is waiting for me there.

Word came from China that his eldest son was ill in hospital with a lung infection, and that one daughter had typhoid fever. His desire to return to China persisted and he went to talk with officials at a government office in London and was given a private interview.

"It is my responsibility to help my family when they are in trouble," he said. "I love them. I would like to go back to China right away. What will happen if I go back?"

He was persuaded for the present to remain in London. Discreet inquiries would be made to see if it were possible for his wife, and those children who wished, to leave China.

On May 3, 1954, he had been in England exactly six years. He read and re-read Psalm 13.

"How long, O Lord? Wilt thou forget me for ever? How long must I bear pain in my soul, and have sorrow in my heart all the day? How long shall my enemy be exalted over me? Consider and answer me, O Lord my God; lighten my eyes, lest I sleep the sleep of death; lest my enemy say, 'I have prevailed over him . . .'"

He had to unburden himself to someone and he wrote to his former student in Norway.

I received a letter from my daughter. She has been improving in health after typhoid fever, but she needs six months convalescence. She did not mention even a word about my family in the north. I can hardly bear any longer the separation from my wife and children. A friend has sent me news that thirty pastors in one area of China were called for investigations. Those who promised never to preach again were told to stand on one side. Two men did this. The other twenty-eight were taken out and shot. I hope this is not true. Nothing has troubled me more than this. Owing to continued hard work my health has suddenly run down. I am in Worthing for a rest.

On the fourth anniversary of the Chinese Church in London, in January 1955, some 150 were present.

PART TWO

"We went through fire and through water,
but thou broughtest us out into a wealthy place."
Psalm 66:12

8

The Pastor's Daughter

I MET STEPHEN'S DAUGHTER, Sung Ling, in 1955 in Shanghai. I was a student in the medical college and she was a lecturer in the Bible seminary. In a year when I was subject to Communist pressure to cleanse my soul by confession, to reject all hostile thoughts about the State, and to lose all love for my family and my old beliefs, meeting her was a beautiful experience. She was twenty-seven, and I was twenty, and much less mature. She was about my height, slightly heavier, gentle, kind and loving, and when she spoke she never raised her voice.

That year I was detained at college during part of the summer vacation for systematic political studies. A convinced Communist, fifteen years older than myself, had given up her holiday to stay with me night and day to expound the benefits of the Chinese revolution. She believed that Communism would conquer the world in her lifetime, and the belief was her inspiration.

There could not have been a greater contrast between this member of the 'Persuasion corps', concerned with political re-education and thought reform, and my new acquaintance Sung Ling.

The chairman of the Protestant Three-Self Movement had said Christians should show a new spirit: 'Love-country, Love-Church', but although Sung Ling did love China and the Church which is the Body of Christ, she preferred to speak of Love-God.

In the medical college, on the flat roof of the School of

Pharmacy, each morning at six up to twenty-five students had gathered to pray. We had arrived silently, picked up a cushion and knelt in twos and threes. These start-of-the-day rendezvous had been discovered and banned by the authorities, but now I had an invitation to go with another medical student to the prayer meeting held in the seminary, and it was there I met Sung Ling.

The prayer gathering was in a large first floor room and it was filled with men and women, both students and staff. I knew, as I heard them pray, that I could not match their spirituality. I was reminded of the early Church prayer meeting when Peter was imprisoned, and earnest prayer for him was made to God by the Church.

Wang Ming-tao, who had firmly refused to compromise with the Communists, had been arrested. As we prayed he was in prison, found guilty of being a counter-revolutionary.

His arrest had struck a fresh note of fear. We found it unbelievable that while this fearless man of God, so widely used, was a prisoner, the Protestant Three-Self Patriotic Movement was declaring that they thanked God for recent years in which the Chinese Church had not only made progress in its spiritual work, but had attained a sense of solidarity which it never had before. The Movement stated that if Christians were patriotic and law-abiding, that the government, under the guarantee of religious liberty would protect the Church, its lawful activities and its proper interests.

In that prayer meeting we knew that God only was our refuge and help.

Sung Ling was courageous but she was rather badly shaken.

"Sister Wang," she asked, "will you pray for me often?"

I was surprised that she asked me, but I did not know how precarious was the future of the staff of the Bible seminary.

"We need constantly to pray for each other," I replied.

She was older than her years, her hair tied tightly in the fashion of many such Christians. She wore traditional Chinese garments, rare in 1955; a long padded dress, covered by a cotton gown which could be washed separately.

After that, whenever we met, she would read a few sentences

from the Bible. We would talk but she did not mention her father
or the Chinese Church in London which, in the political climate,
was understandable. It would be several years before I met
Stephen in Hong Kong, and then I would not identify the
relationship.

She was still in Shanghai, at the seminary, when I reached
Hong Kong on August 3, 1957. On November 29 of that year she
wrote to her father in London.

I think of you so much, especially your health. Winter has
come. Do please take care. I am continually blessed with a
perfect peace in my heart. I received mother's letter. I know
you are anxious about home. I enclose the letter for you.
Grandma is not so well, and longing to see me. Mother also
urges me to return. I have cried very much before the Lord. I
am anxious about them and wish I could return, but the deep
love of the Lord has encircled me and I cannot make the
slightest move. I only ask the Lord to lead me to a much deeper
dedication. In an unusual time the Lord has unusual requests.
He has asked me to offer myself above an ordinary offering. If I
don't I have no peace. Only when I say yes can I rest in him,
and draw strength to go on where he wants me to go, to the
very end.

I am sure in your prayer for me you will understand this,
how I should keep with much trembling the very precious
position given to me for the Gospel.

In the biography of Madam Guyon the last page has the
hymn that she wrote when she was in prison. I have learned to
sing this in the last two years, especially in the recent days
because of my complete offering to God. I have much joy and
courage. I can fully understand how Paul and Silas sang
together in prison. How is your work? Busy? May God bless
you and grant you many converts as that offering to him. Praise
God that when we see the fig tree becomes green we know the
Lord is near. I know all the prophecy will be fulfilled.

Because of her ill-health, if she would not return home to

Peking, Stephen wanted her to try and reach Hong Kong. He wrote to her accordingly.

"The seed of the gospel is sown by God's people and needs to be watered," she replied. "Now we have to water it by life and blood. You are my father and I should listen to you, but it is to be ordained by the Lord himself otherwise."

On April 7, 1958 he wrote to her at the seminary in Shanghai.

My child: The prayer that you offered so many thousand miles away has now become effective. I am able to come down to Hastings from London to hold our Easter conference. Forty-one people are here, and God is in our midst leading us to know him in a deeper way.

I received your letter last week and I praise God for it because it gave me power of resurrection and encouraged me to be more energetic in the preaching of the Gospel. I have been ill for over two months. Day and night I spent in reading the Bible and prayer, mentioning you all by name. I trust God's loving kindness and sufficient grace is upon you. Some time ago your mother wrote. The family is as poor as before. I sent £20 for them and £20 for you. Please let me know when you receive it. Hung is growing both in body and knowledge, and is half a head taller than his brother — oh, that's too tall! I have tried to write to you in the last three weeks but have not succeeded. Tomorrow is Easter. May God's resurrection power fill you.

The letter did not reach Sung Ling. It was eventually returned from Shanghai with a note on the envelope: "the person is not here. Please return."

"She has been arrested, I fear," Stephen told a small group in the Chinese Church in London. "The government has probably taken over the seminary buildings. If she had simply gone away a member of the staff would have written."

The suspense gripped him at night, and sleep became a problem, but most of the Chinese Church were unaware of the burden their pastor carried. He shared it with Sister Gladys Stephenson, but he never mentioned it in the public services of the Church.

No word came from Sung Ling, but news from China in 1958 was that while some Church services and Sunday school classes were being held under watchful supervision, those Christians who had not adequately demonstrated their love of socialism were in jeopardy. Only by actively supporting the Communist party could they obtain protection. The director of the Bureau of Religious Affairs had been a party member for twenty-four years. When he was questioned about Christians in prison he said they were not in prison because they were believers, but because of political crimes.

Both Catholic and Protestant Chinese leaders were tempted to win favour by claiming they had been exploited by imperialists in religious cloaks. Doctors, professors, theologians and evangelists, they said, had gathered secret military, economic and other information from China. Mission funds had been one of the traditional methods used by societies in London and New York to control the Chinese Church.

Sung Ling disappeared during the period of the Great Leap Forward when the whole nation was being mobilised to fresh production goals. The clergy with other 'religious professionals' were instructed to join in the collective effort, and most responded freely. The Christian Churches in one city gathered their members to build a new factory. Their slogan was: "Those who have money contribute money, those who have strength contribute strength, and those who have material contribute material."

Buddhist monks farmed, cut down trees, and stoked furnaces. Protestant ministers and Catholic priests planted orchards and ploughed, breaking off for study sessions. They became known as labour-saving preachers. They said they had moved from the exploiting class to serve their country. Like their congregations they now left home at dawn and returned after dark.

In 1959 the Roman Catholic Archbishop of Shenyang said that for the previous ten years three million Chinese Catholics, had been living a democratic, free and increasingly happy life. Chinese Catholics had a high degree of political fervour and a good production record.

How would Sung Ling have reacted to the call to be a labour-loving worker? Stephen had no doubt she would have responded willingly, and indeed she had done any menial task in the seminary since she first went there.

One of her highly qualified friends there had said: "I thought God wanted me to be a doctor, but if they want me to clean latrines they will be cleaned as they have never been cleaned before."

A year passed without word of her, then a letter came from a former school friend who had escaped from China. The friend and her mother had travelled to the Canton border. The mother was shot and died while escaping, but the daughter reached Hong Kong, where she was hospitalised because of the privation of the long trek south and the shock of her mother's death. As soon as she was fit she wrote to Stephen. He shared the news with one or two.

"My child has been sentenced to ten years' hard labour in a prison camp in China's north-west," he said. "She has tuberculosis of the spine, but she has not stopped witnessing."

With other members of the seminary staff she had been willing to do whatever task the government set her, to bend her back but not her faith. In the labour camp she was undergoing intensive thought-reform.

In 1961 she wrote to an 'aunt' in China. The recipient sent it to Stephen, via an address in Hong Kong. He was overcome with emotion as he read the letter.

I am writing to you that you need not worry. The love and mercy that has poured on me from so many makes me thankful ten thousand times. You and all the loved ones have been so concerned about my illness, often asking whether I need any medicine or money. The way you remembered me during my six months confinement to bed has been the source of joy and comfort. Although this is a very cold district and the living conditions are very hard, these years of labour in various ways have made my body stronger. I am happy.

Since last April I have not been working because of illness. I was allowed to receive treatment in the medical quarters. They

discovered that my spine had several swellings along the lum-
bar region and they gave me streptomycin. The Chinese
medicine had no effect on me. After two months treatment I
have improved. Although the swellings still give me pain they
are not spreading. I can take care of myself in the simple things
and I have much quiet every day, from which I benefit. The
desire of my heart is that I may be more loyal, courageous,
aiming towards the goal and daily rising higher.

Everywhere is frozen and covered with snow but I have
enough clothing. May I ask you please, auntie, to forward this
letter and tell my father that I am well and lack nothing. Often I
think of my father's health. Please take care and may I soon
have the opportunity to return and see you all. May the
blessing of the one who is highest be upon you.

Stephen asked God for two miracles.

He wanted to get Sung Ling out of the labour camp, back to
Shanghai, where she could receive the best medical treatment;
and he wanted God to make it possible for at least his wife to
leave China. He gave himself to prayer.

There were many visitors at the House of Rest where he lived
in north London. One day, in the lounge, he found himself in
conversation with an Anglican vicar in whose Church there was a
prominent member of the Foreign Office in London. He confided
to the vicar about his wife and daughter and the vicar mentioned
the matter to the influential member of his Church who agreed to
take it up on Stephen's behalf.

Stephen planned to go to Hong Kong, where permission would
be sought for his wife to join him. He had no savings to pay the
air fare, not surprising out of a weekly income of £6, out of which
he paid £3 for lodging, but that was a small matter.

He travelled back from a conference at Swanwick with Sister
Gladys, and from Derby to London they shared a railway
compartment to themselves.

"I am going to Hong Kong to get my wife out of China," he
smiled, as the green fields and telegraph poles went by.

"Stephen, how wonderful."

He told her the circumstances.

"As I listened," Sister Gladys recalls, "God told me to go with him!"

"God will provide the fare for you," she said, and then dropped her bombshell. "Stephen, I'm going with you."

Now they needed two fares.

At the House of Rest, quietly trusting God to meet his need, Stephen sat at his untidy desk to put it in some kind of order. There was old correspondence, received over more than ten years, receipted accounts, notices of special services, and sermon outlines. A wastepaper basket was by his side.

As he neared the bottom he pulled out an old pile of letters. There was one envelope dated 1950, never opened, still gummed down. The postmark was Birmingham and the date the day he had received the letter from Peking, which had caused him such sorrow, saying, 'Do not return to China'. In his distress he must have put this aside. Feeling somewhat guilty he now opened it and found it was from the Selly Oak colleges. It was a note of appreciation for the lectures he had given on comparative religions and Chinese history. Unforgivable, he thought, that he had never seen it before and replied. Suddenly, he sat up. The letter went on to say that the colleges were donating his fare back to China. A sum sufficient for this had been sent to the Methodist Missionary Society.

Stephen telephoned the treasurer of the Society, who had long been a true friend. He looked into the records and found a note of the cheque.

"That means," Stephen gasped, "that you have the fare to Hong Kong waiting for me. I'm coming to collect it!"

Sister Gladys, sure that God meant her to accompany him, still had to find her fare. A youth club donated £30 and a number of ex-China missionaries sent her £5. She accompanied Stephen to the BOAC booking office where the ticket clerk said they would return to England via Beirut. They were looking at the map and Beirut seemed close to the Holy Land.

"Could we call in at the Holy Land?" Stephen asked.

"No problem, sir. It is about twenty minutes away."

"I'll go to St. Stephen's Gate," he said, "I've longed to ever since I was a boy."

Among those in the London Church who gave themselves to prayer for the success of the mission were Mr. and Mrs. Fan who also fasted. Stephen dreamed of returning to the House of Rest with his wife, and of knowing that his daughter was free and being cared for. A businessman provided money for the cost of her transport from the north to Shanghai should the authorities approve.

Every member of the Church seemed to have some relative in south-east Asia whom their pastor must see and who could provide hospitality. In high spirits they set out for the journey across the world. Stephen and his ex-China missionary companion were hungry for the sounds and sights of the East.

Their optimism was shaken when they reached Hong Kong. Hundreds of other Chinese families were trying to contact relatives on the mainland, using every human cunning. A mother told them of her two boys, eighteen and twenty, whom she had been praying would be given exit permits. An exhausted youth reached freedom after five hours in the water, but some did not make it. Hope was markedly absent. In every place there was a vast accumulation of non-fulfilment, producing a fantastic strain.

After interminable hours and a thousand nagging irritations, tenuous contact was made with Mrs. Wang through intermediaries. Then began the agonising wait for word from the People's Republic of China. Days passed and shadowy nights. It came in the form of a telegraphed message from his wife: "Unable to travel. High blood pressure."

Bitterness temporarily dulled his exhausted mind. This couldn't be the last word. The chill of fear gripped him.

"If only I could see her," he kept repeating. "If only I could talk with her and know. What does this mean, God?"

He wrote to Fred and Frances Pyke in America to share the bitter news. He went on to tell of the suffering on the Chinese mainland.

A Chinese pastor in Hong Kong told me that his wife and

children in China were suffering from malnutrition resulting in body swellings. She went to the doctor who gave her a prescription for two breads a day from the communal kitchen manager. When one of her relatives came to see her, she gave her one of her breads, which she accepted with warm tears. Food parcels have been poured into China from Hong Kong, but high customs duty has to be paid.

I had asked friends to post food parcels to Peking, but my wife has recently asked us to stop sending any more for the time being. I am greatly concerned at her position.

A more relaxed note followed.

During my stay in Hong Kong I have visited many of our former Church members, also the parents of our present members. I met Rev. David Wang [the author's father], a former student at Yenching school of religion, who for ten years has been the pastor of a Christian and Missionary Alliance Church. He is seventy but looks younger and stronger than myself. His children are independent now. Rev. and Mrs. Wang may come to Paris for three years if we invite them.

Sister Gladys proved a whirlwind of activity and hope, continuing to seek out people who might have influence. As the days passed he became calmer. When he came to speak at the Christian and Missionary Alliance seminary where I was studying, because he had been at school with my father, I was introduced to him.

He told me about the Church in London and of the growth of the Chinese Overseas Christian Mission. The conversation ended with his invitation to London. It was a new thought. Years later he said that God had sent him to Hong Kong to plant it in my mind. It may be so, for on September 22, 1961, I arrived in London to begin my training as a nurse, rather amazed at myself.

Stephen and Sister Gladys left Hong Kong, hardly able to

believe that Sung Ling remained in a labour camp and Mrs.
Wang in Peking. Of his other children there was little news.

Tears stung their eyes as the airport disappeared below, but at
each stopping place on the return journey they experienced
kindness and understanding. Their time in Malaya and Singapore
was strenuous. In two weeks they visited most of the parents of
present members, and contacted ex-members. There were
preaching opportunities and the weather was warm and the
welcome even warmer. Parents were overjoyed at hearing first
hand of their children.

When he was in the Holy Land he stood by the Lake of Galilee,
praying that God would give him a chance to speak from a boat in
the sea to those standing on the shore. His desire was met and he
was allowed to join three fishermen who spoke English. With
their permission he turned to John's Gospel, and from the boat
read how Jesus stood on the shore, and the disciples knew not
that it was Jesus, until after the catching of the multitude of fishes
Peter said, "It is the Lord". He suggested to the fishermen that
they might ask Jesus to send them some big fishes. They offered
him a boat trip.

He went to St. Stephen's Gate, where he spent a long time in
prayer.

He opened his Chinese Bible to the account in the Acts of the
Apostles which he had known since a boy. He read of the great
wonders and signs which Stephen did among the people, of his
arrest and defence before the high priest.

Now when they heard these things they were enraged, and they
ground their teeth against him. But he, full of the Holy Spirit,
gazed into heaven and saw the glory of God, and Jesus standing
at the right hand of God; and he said, "Behold, I see the
heavens opened, and the Son of Man standing at the right hand
of God". But they cried out with a loud voice and stopped their
ears and rushed together upon him. Then they cast him out of
the city and stoned him; and the witnesses laid down their
garments at the feet of a young man named Saul. And as they
were stoning Stephen, he prayed, "Lord Jesus, receive my

spirit". And he knelt down and cried with a loud voice, "Lord, do not hold this sin against them". And when he had said this, he fell asleep.

Stephen looked upwards, with awe and wonder. It was a moment of renewal and resurrection, balanced between Hong Kong and London.

"This is the gate where I got my name," he said to Sister Gladys. "I have never been worthy of it."

On his return to London he found the Church prospering, and there was discussion about the appointment of an assistant pastor. He spent part of that summer ministering on the continent. In Paris "the Holy Spirit worked mightily among the congregation" and there were several conversions. In Holland "we were very busy and tired. There were six conversions according to my record." He was accompanied by two members of the London Church who sacrificed their normal salaries to be with him.

There was also frustration.

"Today I visited many people and found some had grown cold and some had fallen away, which made me very upset and heartbroken. I wish I could stay here for a longer period to build up the work properly but I have no one to help. These are my people, my heart cries for them. If there was a way to push them into the Kingdom of God I would do it. Christ is the way and I want them to know him."

In May 1962, the fourteenth anniversary of his arrival in England, he wrote: "Every year I remember this day. O Lord, how long? Here in Liverpool it is very desolate. We must pray much more and work harder. I will go out to visit very soon, then five days evangelistic meetings at the Malaysian teachers' training college. I thank God I have a much bigger family. I often ask God to grant me a much bigger heart."

9

That Cannot Be Destroyed

FOR HALF A CENTURY Stephen had dreamed of going to America. When he made his first visit he spent five months as a guest in the home of Dr. John Leighton Stuart, missionary educationalist, and from July 1946 American Ambassador to China. Three months after the fall of Nanking to the Communists Dr. Stuart returned to America. President Truman accepted his resignation as Ambassador in December 1952, after he had a severe stroke.

Stephen was grieved to find his former university President paralysed, but was delighted to find a boyhood friend, Philip Fugh, caring for him. They had been students together at Yenching. Philip treated the former Ambassador like a much-loved father, helping him downstairs each day from his bed.

Dr. Stuart and Stephen had a great deal to tell each other and the days sped by. Both knew that the educational institutions to which they had dedicated themselves in China were being used by the Communists. Both knew former colleagues and students who had been indoctrinated and persecuted for their faith. Some had died for making a Christian stand. Although both men had been spared the sufferings, indignities and perils imposed by the Communists, they prayed together for those for whom there had been a heavy cross.

But all was not lost.

Dr. Stuart gave Stephen a copy of his autobiography *Fifty Years in China*.

"I have knowledge too of things that have not been

destroyed, things that cannot be destroyed, things that will not be destroyed," he had written. "In the apparent darkness on the China mainland there burn many lights — lights of faith, of courage, of freedom that will not be extinguished. And among the millions of Chinese overseas, in Chinese communities in Formosa and in many places around the world, the light is shining."

Stephen told his former President of the spiritual needs of the Chinese in Europe, and the old man's eyes lit up as they discussed the possibility of the formation of an American board of the Chinese Overseas Christian Mission, which would provide support, encouragement and fellowship on a generous scale.

When he found that Stephen had, at that time, received little financial support from the British he said, "Why not us?" and introduced Stephen to influential Christian leaders, who could be the first members of his Board. He successfully sought the assistance of Dr. and Mrs. Fred Pyke, and their son Dr. James Pyke, of Wesley Theological Seminary, who were to prove stalwarts.

Daily Stephen prayed and read the Bible with Dr. Stuart.

"Isn't it wonderful," he said, "that one of my former students whom I taught is now reading and explaining the Bible to me. When I am old and sick God has sent you to me. I am so proud of what you are doing in Europe. Yes, I will gladly be the first President of your American Board."

With the Pykes there was a strong bond, for three generations of Pykes had served in China; the grandparents now dead, whom Stephen had met as a boy; Dr. and Mrs Pyke and their son, James.

The senior Pykes introduced the Rev. Donald T. McIntosh, a Methodist Minister, and he was invited on to the board. His years in the pastorate had been marked by a strong emphasis on missionary outreach resulting in vastly increased local missionary giving as well as a good number of young people giving their lives for full-time Christian service. Out of this experience, he had been privileged to help a number of other Churches to establish strong local missionary programmes. He had travelled extensively throughout many areas of the world, observing the various facets of missionary endeavour as well as ministering to both missionaries and nationals.

Stephen was attracted to him and his gifted wife, Evelyn. Their ministry had been influenced initially by that of Dr. Oswald J. Smith of Toronto, a legendary figure in missionary circles. The contribution to the C.O.C.M. of Donald and Evelyn McIntosh was to be considerable. Apart from their evangelistic work their responsibility for fund-raising was to have its own strains, but they possessed ever-increasing zeal.

The special task in the United States was to arouse an awareness, a responsibility, and a sense of privilege in having a part in the ministry of making Christ known, especially to the many thousands of Chinese in Britain and on the Continent.

Stephen was moved by the closeness of the relationship between Dr. Stuart and Philip Fugh. For years his former school friend had stood by the American, assisting in his release from detention by the Japanese army, accompanying him to the United States in August 1949, and hurrying to his side when he had a stroke. The friendship, based on perfect trust, had lasted forty years.

"Philip, you are closer than a son," Stephen told him.

"I'm also his companion, secretary and public relations officer," Philip laughed.

When the doctors said that no one, except a close member of the family could be with Dr. Stuart for more than ten minutes, they allowed Philip to spend hours with him. During his five months in hospital Philip did not miss seeing him on a single day, and they shared their home together.

It was a unique American-Chinese friendship, enriching to both. Like Philip, Stephen held the Americans in high esteem, and in Peking had benefited from their generosity. Now he saw the way American Christians had been taught to give and believed this was something the rest of the world should share.

"The Chinese have much to learn in this matter," he told Philip, when he learned how thousands of dollars were raised by children.

When he addressed American Churches he thanked them for their support over many years of Chinese educational institutions, churches and hospitals. He thanked them too for the missionaries they had sent to China during 140 years of Protestant missions;

missionaries who had known ill-health, famine, misunderstanding, terrorism; who had been dispossessed of their belongings and restricted in their movement.

"Why did the Communists throw us out?" he was asked. "Why the skilful propaganda which made your people turn against missionaries, particularly American ones?"

It was a situation he could not deny for some missionaries had been identified with politicians and with American grants for Rural Reconstruction.

Stephen knew that although Communist propaganda might cause distress to hundreds of missionaries who had lived sacrificially, that there were lessons to be learned from such accusations. Some missionaries had not lived like the people who dwelt there, and had not really been involved in their lives.

"I have a sense of shame myself," he confessed, "for I identified myself with Western living standards, demanding a missionary rate of pay for being headmaster, when my example should have been Christ. From a humble home I set my sights on material advantages when I should have used my education solely to serve my people."

He refuted as nonsense any blanket condemnation of missionaries, but accepted that men of all nations have, as always, misrepresented Christ. This must not, he insisted, result in the Church ceasing to be missionary-minded.

He met many Chinese in America and gave some assistance in the way of inspiration in the formation of the Chinese Church in Washington D.C. This thriving Church is quite independent and self-supporting. The group he met in Washington on his first visit, mainly students, heard of the Church in London, but soon their Church was to outgrow its European counterpart.

On his return to London Stephen decided that he must no longer draw an income from the Methodist Missionary Society, but that the work should be completely independent of any denomination. A few of his Methodist friends were saddened by this decision.

"I will always be a *Chinese* Methodist," Stephen said. "I thank God for the Methodists."

"We must not try to keep Stephen Wang in the Methodist mould," a senior Methodist said. "Wherever the Chinese people are he must be free to go. God's blessing will go with him."

In autumn 1962, a letter came from America telling of the death of Dr. Stuart, almost his oldest Methodist friend. His testimony was that he had found "Jesus Christ as sublimely satisfying in my old age as in my youth. He has my absolute reverence and devotion."

An evangelical doctrinal basis was agreed for the interdenominational work. It said: We believe in the divine inspiration of the Holy Scriptures as authority in matters of faith and conduct. The unity of the Father, the Son and the Holy Spirit in the Godhead. The universal sinfulness and guilt of human nature. Redemption from the guilt, penalty and power of sin only through the sacrificial death of Jesus Christ the Incarnate Son of God. The resurrection of Jesus Christ from the dead. The necessity of the work of the Holy Spirit to make the death of Christ effective to the individual sinner, granting him repentance towards God and faith in Jesus Christ. The indwelling and work of the Holy Spirit in the believer. The expectation of the personal return of the Lord Jesus.

Not all who worshipped in the Church necessarily accepted all the doctrinal basis, but it was maintained in the ministry.

Stephen all these years had been living at the House of Rest. There he had been blessed with companionship and love. A regular visitor was Mary Chu who arrived in London in 1953, professedly an atheist. Under Stephen's ministry she found Christ. When he was ill for four months she called at the House of Rest every day to cook for him between her studies as a physiotherapist.

"Nobody is perfect in this world," Stephen said, "but Mary Chu almost."

She was to marry Charles Tang. Charles came from a wealthy family and was something of a playboy when he arrived in London to study architecture. Wandering about the streets, knowing no one, he was gripped on the shoulder in friendly fashion one day and invited to an Inter-Varsity Fellowship gathering. The I.V.F. were conducting a welcome campaign for foreign students and they introduced Charles to the Chinese

Church. He had a glorious conversion and almost immediately afterwards started to preach, never bothered if he made a mistake. He accompanied Stephen to the continent and later returned to Holland to assist Sister Van Zeijl in Rotterdam, who had a great love for the Chinese. His spiritual zeal never cooled and there was rejoicing when he and Mary married. They are now in Malaya.

Molly Soo was a resident in the House of Rest. At night she would prepare a pot of Chinese porridge on the gas ring ready for Stephen's return. It was a domestic break from her studies at the London Bible College. Now she is active in the C.O.C.M. in Holland where her husband is a scientist.

It was my great gain to be another of Stephen's daughters, although I could never be a Mary Chu, a Molly Soo or a King Ling. He started his letters to me with either 'my dear child' or 'my dear daughter'. Soon after my arrival in London he wrote: "In you, I see something of my dear Sung Ling. God has so planned, that you can be with me while she can't. How gracious he is to me. In all our trials and suffering we can experience his sufficient grace."

I was so grateful to God that I had known Sung Ling in Shanghai, even though for a comparatively short time, but by her I was a person of small stature, afraid to consider how I might have faced up to years in a labour camp. From a source which has to remain anonymous we had heard how because of her firm stand she had been isolated from friends and relatives outside the camp at a period when others were allowed occasional visitors.

In the prologue I have told of my visit to Stephen when he was on holiday in Colchester, and of my promise to stand with him in the work while ever he needed me. This I believed was why God had allowed me to escape from China. It was after this holiday that he wrote:

My dear daughter: Since my God is your God we must serve him together so that we may receive his blessings. The work he has given us we must accomplish with the same mind and heart. Let us stand on the word of the Lord to seek first his Kingdom and his righteousness; in everything seeking God's

will so that we may receive power to 'push' the work of God
forward. In everything we must seek unity and co-operation
from all the brothers and sisters and work together with them. I
admire the determination of Ruth in the Old Testament; her
courage and her single-minded devotion, but I respect more
Mary, when she broke the precious jar of alabaster ointment
and quietly gave all to the Lord. With her sympathy and
encouragement she stood by the Lord Jesus in his most worthy
commission. I thank God for you and I know your giving is the
beginning of receiving. Your loving uncle.

An appeal was launched to purchase a Chinese Church centre, in
Hollywood Road, London, for £10,000 and gifts came from many
parts of south-east Asia, from the continent, but mostly from the
Chinese in London. When completion date came £3,000 was
loaned by Christians to make up the £10,000. A year later, on
Stephen's sixty-fifth birthday, always a major occasion for the
Chinese, he was asked what he would like as a present, some
clothes or books maybe.

"You really want to know what I would like?" he asked. "My
desire is to pay off the £3,000 for the building."

The young people sent a letter to scattered members overseas
and to those at home explaining the gift was not for himself but for
the Church. Cheques and money orders started to flow in and
everyday he was in the office counting the total. Someone who had
loaned £1,000 wrote and said it need not be repaid. Finally, some
£4,000 was received.

Sunday services continued in the central Y.M.C.A. but the
Chinese centre which was opened in June 1964 by Bishop
Houghton, was considered to be 'Chinese soil'. For many nurses
and students it became a spiritual birthplace and a home, and
Stephen, as a father-figure, took up residence, making himself
available day and night. Burdens were shared as young visitors
discovered his capacity for warm-hearted sympathy. "I will pray
for you daily," he promised and he did. Whatever the emotional
tension they were soon relaxed in his presence and usually left
exhilarated and with a stronger faith. When young men came to

him with moral difficulties he was understanding and loving, but always he firmly upheld God's standards. Often the problem was loneliness resulting in depression. "In the morning thou shalt say, Would God it were even! and at even thou shalt say, Would God it were morning!" (Deut. 28:67). An hour with him meant for hundreds a turning point. He was more than three times the age of many he counselled, and this could have been an obstacle, but it rarely proved that way.

"He introduced me to Christ," many testified after a meal or an evening at the centre. His ability to influence young people was enormous, and can only be explained by the statement that God used him. There is no other single explanation.

Between March 1963 and November 3, 1964 Sung Ling was able to write several letters. The letters did not say, but Stephen believed, that she had been for a while among three million people, mostly women, who were employed cutting down trees and making roads into Tibet.

On a small scrap of paper came the following note to Auntie, dated March 19.

I received the two parcels you sent to me containing food and soap. I am thankful because in a hundred different ways you have put your heart and strength to take care of me. Such love and graciousness challenge me daily to climb up higher, but may I request most earnestly that from now on you keep all the food for yourself. You are elderly and your health has always been poor and there is no one to take care of you. Even so, year after year you worry and think of me. I am not worthy. You must have more nutritious food to improve your health and that will make me happy. The parcels that Mien sent to the factory for me have been received by others. Please do not worry.

My health is improving. The swelling around my waist is subsiding, but the disease has affected my upper spine, and my shoulder bones give me pain. Your continued remembrance will make me blessed a hundredfold.

I will be allowed to return to the factory to work again when transport is available. I have improved from the condition which

for the past year or so has made me at times semi-conscious and
for this I am thankful. I received your letter written in January
and I trust you received my letter sent in February. I will write
again after I return to the factory.

On April 4, 1963 came the following.

At the end of March I received your two letters. I wrote to you
on March 19 acknowledging your two parcels. I trust you
received it. Regarding the parcel you sent on March 1, containing material and clothing, was this sent to the factory? The
people in charge there have written saying they would take care
of any parcels. I am improving and the doctor will allow me to
return to work, but I am still waiting for transport. Next time
when you send parcels to me you only need mention how many
items and not what they are. I will receive them safely.

I was told that Sister Mai is working. Her health is good, so
you should not be anxious. I don't need to tell you more. You
must take care of yourself and keep the food for yourself. Will
you promise me so that I do not need to be anxious about you?

I have enough money. There is nothing I can buy here. You
said you wished to send me a blanket-cover which would be
wonderful, but there is no need to hurry. I have enough. I can
get up every day and take care of the small things for myself.
The quiet and rest has benefited me. Very unfortunately, this
paper is so small that I cannot tell you much, but I am bathing
in grace because of your remembrance. I will write again after I
return to the factory. I can never express my appreciation. I
only hope that you will be rewarded because of your labour for
me.

Peace! [said a letter dated April 2, 1964]. Has your health been
good lately? You are getting old therefore you must pay attention to your diet. I received your letter written on March 10
and all the parcels you sent to me. Now I can buy the extras I
need and I have enough. Please do not send so much to me
especially biscuits which occupy so much space. Also do not

send me medicine. All my needs are sufficiently supplied. I work in one of the factory sections and the labour is not too hard. I know to encourage myself to go forward. I hope to hear from you after you receive this letter to let me know that you are well so that my heart can rest.

Dear Aunt [started her note on May 2, 1964], I am anxious about you. I am worried because I did not hear from you in April. Your letter in March and parcels containing flour and beans were received safely and I am grateful. Did you receive my letters in March and April? Please don't send any more things to me because it is better for me not to receive. I have sufficient. You must not save things for me because you are old and you need extra nutrition. I suppose the children have all gone to school one by one and there is much you have to provide for them. I have offered thanksgiving ten thousand times because of your labour. My work is not too heavy. I have sufficient strength and I live happily. I know how to encourage myself. I heard that old grandpa [probably a reference to Dr. Chia] has died, but I know nothing more and I am concerned.

On June 1, 1964, she wrote:

I received your letter dated May 6. I am greatly comforted because you are well. I trust I shall receive your parcels. I received the food coupons you sent last winter and the extra coupons for three more pounds of food. I have only used half a pound. Please do not send any more; I have medicine but I can't take it because it upsets my stomach.

In July I shall write to my mother because my youngest brother will be graduating from university, and it will be father's sixty-fifth birthday. These are two big and happy occasions. May my parents be blessed with long life. We younger people surely should be happy and congratulate them.

Your labour for me for so many years and your encouragement that I may continue to grow in love is a great comfort to my parents. Although my spine gives me much pain I am resting with peace of heart and live full of hope. Last month it was possible for me to buy soap powder, toilet paper, and a glass, all things which I could not buy before. I lack nothing. Keep them for yourself and the children and this will please me. Write when you can.

The last letter received was dated November 3, 1964. It was addressed to a friend in Shanghai who had been released from a labour camp.

I received your letter dated September 27 and the photographs of the three children. I am delighted that they have grown so big and well. It took me a while to know who is who. I recall when they were born, their little red faces, and how they slept so sweetly when they were taken to the photographers. I remember the joy for me to hold their little hands to write to you [when the recipient was in prison, Sung Ling before her own arrest, cared for them]. Suddenly they have grown up and they can continue the desire of their parents and aim to accomplish their work. I congratulate you. How I hope that you will encourage and help them in their spare time, teaching them to memorise the old book and explaining to them carefully. Such time spent in learning will benefit their entire life. It has been my longing to study more language in order to be able to dig deeper into the old book but now I am very ill in prison and I can study no more. Encourage the three children so that in coming days they might fulfil my ambition and desire.

I know that you and your husband are in haulage. Take care and do not overwork. Do the children have winter clothes and boots? How are your living conditions? Remember we should rejoice, looking up — if we expect blessings we shall surely receive them that our lives may be richer.

I can no longer work. Apart from the many swellings the top of my spine, around the neck, is very painful. I have been x-rayed and need to return to find the result. I will be given treatment if the authorities think it necessary. I have lost much weight in the last few months, but my inner strength is sufficient.

Let your heart be at rest. Ultimately, it will be good after all these various trials and testings. I am sorry I did not write to you in the last three months and for the anxiety this caused. Lately, I have written to my aunt. I was glad I was able to write because for some months I have caused her much worry. The living conditions here have improved. I am able to buy some extras and daily necessities. I have enough in food and clothing. My only desire is that you will take care of yourself and enjoy peace and contentment.

Stephen came to believe that Sung Ling died a few months later. "She was my dearest child," he confessed, looking at her photograph. "She was found worthy to suffer for Christ."

10

The Outreach

"IN GERRARD STREET, in the middle of modern metropolitan London, there is now a Chinatown," reported the *Daily Telegraph*.

It began with the restaurants. Today there are Chinese barbers, Chinese beauty parlours, Chinese mini-cabs, accountants, bookshops and libraries, supermarkets, travel-agents, gambling clubs and even a chamber of trade . . . Sociologically the community is incredible. Many of the Chinese who frequent it may not have spoken to an Englishman. Many will not even speak English. In one of its most prominent restaurants out of a staff of seventeen there are fourteen who can speak no English at all. The community flourishes, a little island lapped by the acres of London.

In 1951 there were some 4,800 Chinese in Britain. Today the figure is estimated to be more than 58,000, of whom more than eighty per cent are in the restaurant business. Most of the restaurants open at mid-day for lunch and close at midnight or later. The staff have a couple of hours off in the afternoon, and may have Monday or Tuesday as their day off. There are a few Communists among them, and it is possible to buy a party newspaper from a Maoist supporter, but most of the Chinese are busy making a living and show no interest in ideology.

The C.O.C.M. outreach is illustrated by Frank Cheung. Frank came from Hong Kong in 1960 and found a restaurant job two minutes from Gerrard Street, in an English restaurant in Dean Street among the striptease clubs. In Canton his family were Buddhists, worshipping their ancestors around the altar in their home. As a boy he daily used to ask his dead grandfather for his blessing. If his mother beat him he prayed that grandfather would stop her; if his lessons were difficult he turned to his grandfather for inspiration. In 1948 he left mainland China with his father who started a tailoring business in Hong Kong. Mother was to follow when grandmother died, but when she died in 1964 it was impossible for her to leave.

In 1955 Frank was taken on Easter Sunday to the Holy Light church in Hong Kong. It was the second church service he had ever attended, the first being a Roman Catholic one when he accompanied his grandmother. Because he showed a lack of respect to God by falling asleep grandmother did not take him again. In Canton he had never met a Protestant and he did not know what a missionary looked like.

The Easter congregation numbered seventy, and Frank was impressed by the sincerity of the Chinese pastor, and the happy atmosphere. He was invited to go again. He compared what he learned with Buddhism and asked some penetrating questions.

He became a Christian a few days before Christmas 1955, and a few months later, with sixteen others, was baptised. His father objected strenuously, speaking derisively of the foreign religion, and keeping him busy in the tailor's shop on Sundays. While his father gambled he was able to slip out for a church service.

When he arrived in England, two years after his brother, seeking better prospects, he had every intention of maintaining his Christian links. It proved difficult. He found his way to a large Anglican church but the form of service was strange and his English was poor. Sunday work in the restaurant and the long hours gradually made him lose touch. From London he went to Birmingham, then to Coventry, Nottingham and back to Birmingham. Sometimes he opened his Bible and prayed, but for three years did not attend a church service.

In 1964 he was co-proprietor of a Birmingham Chinese restaurant which was visited by a student from the Birmingham Bible Institute. The student discovered that he had been baptised and wrote to Pastor Wang who was soon on the train from London. After the busy lunch period he entered the restaurant and introduced himself. It was Frank's first contact with the Chinese Overseas Christian Mission, and the Pastor of the London Church.

"I was so happy to see him," Frank recalls. "I told him to sit down and I brought some tea. He told me about his work and where he came from. I asked how he knew about me, and he explained about the Bible college student."

"Any brothers and sisters?" Stephen asked.

"Yes, thirteen! But I'm the only one who is a Christian."

Pastor introduced him to Chinese Christians in Birmingham and they started to meet together for a monthly fellowship in his restaurant basement. There were fourteen at the first meeting. Frank soon found himself re-established in the faith, encouraged by teams of Chinese nurses and students, accompanied by Pastor, who came from London for special occasions.

In 1965 he met Chi Ching, a lovely Chinese nurse at the Marsden Green hospital, who had arrived in England from Hong Kong in 1964. Pastor gave the bride away at the wedding.

In 1967 he became part-owner of a very profitable restaurant in Stratford-on-Avon, but that year he faced a spiritual crisis. It occurred when his father died and he paid a quick visit to Hong Kong. He had often written urging his father to become a Christian, but he always replied that he would consider it in the future. He died unexpectedly of a brain haemorrhage. He had withheld nothing of himself in the race for prosperity, and the words of Jesus came to Frank. "What shall it profit a man if he gain the whole world and lose his own soul?" He saw himself, like his father, working non-stop for forty years, seven days a week.

On his return he was challenged by a sermon preached by Stephen from John's Gospel where Jesus said to Peter: "Lovest thou me more than these?" At an International Conference of the C.O.C.M. when they discussed the need for two men to give themselves exclusively to restaurant evangelism he believed God was calling him. From his own bitter experience he saw the need.

He discussed it with his wife and in February 1969 he parted with his share in the restaurant to give himself. He knew the Chinese restaurants in Birmingham, some of them for seven years, but his commission was to visit every Chinese restaurant in Britain. An impossible task! Bible studies were started in restaurants in the afternoons, non-Christians sitting in and listening with quiet respect.

Stephen accompanied him on several non-stop programmes, morning till night. Although Stephen spoke only Mandarin and not Cantonese the waiters showed him the traditional respect which they show to the elderly, and Frank learned, by example, how to reach men for Christ.

On his first Monday Frank met with encouragement. A waiter said, "I am miserable and would like to live a better life. Tell me more?"

Ko Tin-sing was in his early twenties and they met on his day off, sitting in the reading room of the public library in Dudley. He became a Christian and brought a friend to Frank who was in trouble. He too found Christ.

Frank visited four hundred restaurants in his first year, speaking either Cantonese or Mandarin. There were then two thousand Chinese restaurants in Britain: by 1972 there were 2,500 with new ones opening weekly.

In 1971 he visited Washington and New York to tell of his mission, and to examine what was being done there. He also examined similar ministries on the Continent.

Stephen was as concerned about Chinese students and professional men in Europe as about the waiters.

A writer in *International Students* wrote about the C.O.C.M.:

The organisation has its prime work among Chinese trainees and professional people in the great centres of Britain and western Europe. Through its ministry hundreds of these high-level personnel are led to a saving faith in Jesus Christ. Many, after growth in spiritual things, see their own homeland as a great field 'white unto harvest'. They hear the Spirit of God speak to them about proclaiming the Gospel to their own countrymen. As they muse, the fires burn. Before long they have prepared themselves. They return on their own to their homeland (where the millions of Chinese live and have their influence), enthusiastically bearing the Gospel tidings. Of course, it would be presumptuous to say that the majority become pastors and evangelists. Others go back as nurses and doctors or technicians or to assume some responsible government post. While some are able to penetrate the Bamboo Curtain bearing the Gospel, others work in areas where the foreign missionary for one reason or another is forbidden or is not readily received. An educated national gets a better audience among the Chinese.

The reason for this is simple. First of all, he does not have to become un-American or un-English to be received by the people. He knows the language, the customs, the taboos. He can live as a country-man among the Chinese — eating their food, keeping within their economic framework. The Englishman or the American will encounter difficulties on all these counts and in the process consume two to four years learning the language, along with a large amount of money and, when all this is done, still not be as effective as the national sold out to God. On this principle C.O.C.M. is working. And on this principle the Church of Christ is going forward in areas that are even closed to Western missionaries.

Pastor was given a vision of evangelising south-east Asia, but his vision did not exclude foreign missionary service. At a summer conference fifty young people rose to dedicate themselves as messengers to proclaim God's love to their own people when they returned home professionally qualified. So the field was widened to embrace not only Europe but also south-east Asia.

"We believe," Pastor said, "that south-east Asia can best be evangelised by ourselves because it is our own home. Pray that God will thrust forth our people to be witnesses in this field."

From those returning to Asia from London came encouraging news.

"Among the Asians we have formed a youth group and we meet once a week for Bible study, 'singspiration' and games. We run a Bible course for our members too."

"I am teaching in Kampong Kuantan, forty-two miles from Kuala Lumpur (capital of Malaya)," another wrote. "The majority of the pupils are Indians and a few of them are Roman Catholics. They have hardly heard the name of Jesus and I take the opportunity to tell them of him and of his wonderful love for us."

Mr. Chua Wee-hian was assistant pastor of the Chinese Church in London in the early sixties. He returned in 1970 as Associate General Secretary of the I.F.E.S. (Far East) to speak at a C.O.C.M. Leadership Training Conference in London. He told how the Asian Churches are small flickers of light in a land mass of darkness. Although the Gospel had been preached in Asia for more than a century, Christians at most numbered four per cent of the population, including many nominal ones.

"The light of the Gospel is threatened by resurgent religions. Buddhism and Hinduism have appeared in new guise. The Sokagakkai in Japan claim to have a membership of five million families. The Muslims have their own missionary training centres. Communism has trampled the Christian faith in China and it will not tolerate the exclusive claims of Christ."

He said there was a need for vocational witness where God calls his men and women to demonstrate his reality, the standards of Christian ethics, the outworking of Christian love in all spheres of life service.

In some cases, some of these vocational witnesses have made a greater impact than Western missionaries. Through their professions, they can identify themselves with people and they can make vital contacts with key non-Christians. I have known some who have started Christian centres, assisted in weak and struggling local Churches and God has prospered their witness and mission. Many of you will be returning to the Far East, some to former Churches, others to new ones. Play your part in these Churches. Go with a sense of service and please be slow to criticise. You cannot find an exact replica of the Chinese Church in London in Asia!

Christian living is important. I would like to make a strong plea for open Christian homes. Ninety per cent of Asians have no concept of what a Christian home is. Most of them have never been to one. There is a definite place for frank and practical discussions of Christian marriage and family life. If God ever gives you a home, I hope that it will be an open one.

The other area of witness is the full-time ministry. I do not believe that this is 'Grade A' and 'Division 1' where Christian service is concerned. But God in his grace will call some to give their lives for this strategic task. Our Churches need godly men to give spiritual leadership and to teach the whole counsel of God.

This is not an easy age to live in. God has never called us to relative security and popularity. But when he summons, it is our task to obey, to find out where he wants us to be. Above all, we must not waste our lives in purposeless pursuits. We must be available for him. But right now, we prepare, by faithful training through the disciplined study of his word, the daring outreach to non-Christians.

"Amen, amen," said Stephen. He constantly spoke of the temptations which faced a qualified Chinese Christian returning to Asia.

Increasingly, the heart can become the slave of the flesh, leading to greed and the quest for money. The love of money is the root of all evil, and those who covet money pierce themselves with many sorrows. They pierce the inner man, not the outer man, and the inner man suffers. This suffering of the inner man inevitably affects the outer man, since inner and outer are one person.

I accompanied Stephen to America in 1966. It was a fruitful

visit, culminating in an offer from the States to support me financially in work among the thousands of Chinese nurses in Britain. I had passed my nursing examinations, and now I joined the staff of C.O.C.M. for this specialised task, after some hesitation about my ability, and a discussion with the hospital matron in London. In some hospitals in Britain there were as many Chinese as English nurses, and few hospitals had less than a score of Chinese girls. They were from Singapore, Malaysia and Hong Kong, and had raised their own fare.

Stephen found that many could not speak much English and were disinclined off duty to mix with other nationalities. They often shut themselves in their rooms, desperately lonely, although certain enlightened matrons went out of their way to draw them into community life. Stephen saw this ministry as being as necessary as restaurant or student contact.

Holidays presented a problem for the nurses. Most could not afford to return to Asia until their training was complete. The Chinese centre at Hollywood Road offered temporary accommodation for a few girls, others were able to arrange their holidays to coincide with our conferences, but only the fringe of the need was being met. I was appointed to speak to spiritual needs but these cannot be isolated from domestic and personal problems and increasingly I was asked to speak to matron or sister on some matter.

Soon I was in touch with more than one thousand nurses. I found that a big percentage described themselves as Buddhist, although this was frequently a nominal family religion. About five per cent had a Christian background. I introduced them to the Chinese Church and to the various fellowships scattered through Britain. Far from home, Stephen became a father-figure to them, listening, advising, writing to parents and friends in Asia at their request.

Because I had been separated from my parents for several years, because I had arrived in England, rather nervous, to train as a nurse, because my experience was so close to theirs, I was able to get close to the girls.

It was not by accident that Stephen selected for the restaurants Frank who had been a waiter, and for the hospitals one who had been a nurse. There were problems to which I did not know the solution, sometimes involving a Chinese nurse and a ward sister who seemed incompatible, and I was able to draw on his experience as headmaster and pastor. I also learned from the nurses.

There were girls who knew they had chosen the wrong profession. It was easy for an English girl to give up and return home to be a secretary or housewife, but the Chinese girl, with a labour permit, could not switch jobs so easily, or return home to Singapore when she was depressed. In this trying situation there was inner strain, revealing itself in odd ways.

On the whole however the Chinese nurses were fulfilled and dedicated, enjoying excellent relationships with patients and other staff, although drained after long hours. Sitting in their own rooms or together in a fellowship meeting many responded to the call of Christ.

Miss Kwei Lan-liew, who had completed her nurse's training at King Edward Memorial Hospital, Ealing, was appointed to a ministry among the nurses in January 1969. When she went to London Bible College in 1971 her work was taken over by Miss Martha See, another qualified nurse who had done Bible training at Mount Hermon. Without the American Board these appointments would have been impossible.

The Rev. Donald McIntosh in America had served in the pastorate as a member of the Baltimore Conference of the United Methodist Church, In the early sixties his Church, St. John's Methodist, had given him leave to go on a world tour to visit the places which the Church supported. When he returned to America he told the Church that he had not seen anything to equal Stephen's ministry among the Chinese. After this Mr. McIntosh agreed to be the Chairman of the American Board from 1964. On June 15, 1969, his Bishop gave him special appointment to work full-time with the American Board of C.O.C.M.

From him Stephen learned of the Faith Promise Scheme which he introduced to the Chinese Church in London. The outcome was that the London Church, apart from being self-supporting, was able to contribute to the wider activities of the C.O.C.M.

Stephen visited the Paris Church whenever possible. A member of that Church told how he had known Stephen since he went to Paris in 1955 to celebrate Christmas.

In 1957 Pastor Wang held Gospel meetings. On that day I heard the Gospel and accepted Jesus Christ. That night after Pastor Wang had returned to the hotel, a friend told me that although many came to the meeting, not a single one had truly believed in God, and that it was impossible for him to establish a Church in Paris.

The Paris Church has now been established fourteen years. The beginning was as difficult as planting sycamore trees on rocks. As the days went by the number of Christians from mainland China, Taiwan, Hong Kong, Vietnam and Cambodia increased and the Church was formed. Now it is pressing forward, growing, expanding, and evangelising.

Another member of the Paris Church had been introduced to Stephen by Gladys Aylward in England in 1953.

"In 1962 I left England and settled in France. Pastor Wang was in England most of the time, but he was still very concerned about me. Whenever he came to France, he let me have the privilege of having a personal talk with him. I sought his guidance and advice whenever I encountered any difficulties in spiritual or worldly matters."

"He taught me to study Psalm 34:14: 'Depart from evil and do good; seek peace and pursue it'," recalls another member. "No matter how busy he was, whenever he met people with yellow skin, regardless of whether they were strangers, he went forward and spoke to them and presented the Gospel. I have been cheated by people throughout my life, but he was a faithful friend. He was the first person, apart from Jesus Christ, who has been so kind to me."

"He encouraged me to study diligently and to serve God with other young people," wrote a delegate from the Church in Paris to

the London Leadership Training and Summer Conference. "He
wanted me to make use of my study and research in Chinese music
to compile or create a hymnal with Chinese melody accompanied
by musical instruments."

"At first," says another, "there were only two or three brothers
gathered together when Pastor Wang came to Paris, but he was
not discouraged. On his last visit to Paris he told me lovingly how
he wished he could stay with us, because the Church was like a
big family. The blessing God had granted to it was far beyond his
expectation."

An international conference of the C.O.C.M. was held in
London in January 1968. The Rev. George Scott presided at each
session and there were representatives from the U.S.A., Holland,
Paris, Birmingham, Manchester, and St. Albans. Stephen gave an
encouraging report, covering in brief the whole of the work.
There had been many conversions in England and on the continent. Four ladies had entered Bible college during the year. He
expressed a sense of deep gratitude to God for the financial
support received, particularly that from the U.S.A. Board. During the year thirty-six hospitals had been visited and some 871
nurses contacted. At the monthly meeting of nurses at the centre
there was an average attendance of fifty. Within this period there
had been forty-two professed conversions. There was an urgent
need for more adequate hostel accommodation for nurses on
leave, some having even slept on the floor at the centre. Over
one hundred requests for such accommodation had had to be
refused.

Samuel Chan told of the formation of a choir in London, and
Paul Quek reported that there were now more than one thousand
Chinese, mostly students, in Manchester. From Paris Chen Jia-jer
told of the search for a permanent church building, and John
Chen from Holland spoke of a need for Bibles and hymnbooks in
Chinese. Donald McIntosh elaborated on the needs of the work as
seen by the U.S.A. Board. He hoped for another staff worker
among the nurses, a full-time worker among university students, a
new centre in London, also a centre in Manchester. He wondered
whether someone might soon succeed Stephen as pastor of the

Chinese Church, freeing him to give all his time, thought and energy as director of the C.O.C.M. He closed the conference with a meditation on the need to go forward in faith.

"God tells us to go forward; God does not just ask us to go. He *tells* us to go," he said.

On May 3, 1968, Stephen wrote:

Today is exactly twenty years since I first arrived in England. I will be speaking to the medical students who are preparing themselves for missionary work, at noon today. Tomorrow I will travel up to Manchester to officiate at a Chinese wedding, and the next day I will preach at two services; one for the Cantonese speaking through interpretation to the restaurant workers, and the other to the Chinese Christian fellowship. On May 7 I will go to Scotland to speak at different churches until the 19th. No news from China.

During a missionary week organised by the Cambridge Christian Union in 1968 Stephen was the missioner for Asian overseas students. A law student at Jesus College accepted Christ and Stephen returned to visit him several times. "I would very much like to meet you again, on your next visit to Cambridge," wrote the student. "In the meantime, may I just add that this new life with Christ has opened up an entirely sincere horizon in my everyday living."

In 1969 Stephen spent six weeks in South Africa at the invitation of the Baptist Churches. The invitation had originally been made eight or nine years before, but was renewed when a young South African born Chinese, Arthur Song, trained in the Baptist college, was about to graduate to work among the Chinese.

"I am very busy," he told the London council, "but I do not know how long I have got left to continue my work. If you think it would be a privilege to send your pastor to minister to the Chinese in South Africa, then I am willing to go."

He went to South Africa House, and found it was in the balance as to whether his visit was permissible because of his colour. A visa was granted and he arrived to conduct the Deeper Life Crusade for nine days in Johannesburg. This was for deeper life in believing, deeper life in Bible reading, in praying, in witnessing, in giving and in dedication.

Almost every night in his services there were conversions, among both white and coloured people. He had asked for an undertaking that there would be no discrimination.

Pastor Song saw Stephen "as a modern Paul to the Chinese" and there soon existed a Paul-Timothy relationship between the two men. They visited Pretoria, Port Elizabeth, Capetown, and other large cities, speaking to the Chinese and to community leaders. Pastor Song found Stephen was just as at home with an ambassador as with the coloured primary children who flocked around him.

He encouraged Pastor Song to spend a year in Hong Kong learning Cantonese, and a month in London.

"You have a much greater advantage than I ever had," Stephen told him. "A far greater advantage."

Pastor Song looked surprised.

"I am nothing," he said.

"You are twenty years younger than when I started my ministry in London," Stephen told him. "That is a very great advantage."

The Chinese Baptist Church in Johannesburg, where he ministers, grows steadily. It was born as an outcome of the ministry of Mr. and Mrs. H. W. Pudney. In Capetown there is a Chinese Christian fellowship born as an outcome of Stephen's visit, with a committee of Chinese and Europeans, the Rev. Glyn Tudor, of the Observatory Baptist Church, taking considerable initiative. Stephen spent two profitable weeks in his home.

At Christmas the B.B.C. invited him to broadcast from London to his own people in the Far East. The broadcast was not beamed to China, although some could have heard it. His family were in his mind as he sat before the microphone.

The wise men were from the Far East. It is rather a coincidence that the Chinese character for star is composed of two characters, which are 'birth' and 'day'. When they are put together they become the character for star. At whose birthday was there a star in the sky? When Jesus was born a brilliant star appeared in the east. The wise men not only understood the star, but they also followed it, travelling a long way with gifts for Christ the King.

It is interesting to note that when the wise men came to the capital Jerusalem, they lost sight of their star and were compelled to ask King Herod about the birth-place of Christ. People easily lose their light in the big cities. Quite a number of students who went to study in large cities of the world have lost their religious zeal and faith ... Our desire is that the star of the advent of Jesus will appear again this Christmas, to guide many men of the east to come to Jesus and worship him.

There was a response from many nations, but none from mainland China. The last letter from his family came in 1965. He did not know if his wife was still alive. He was consoled by the knowledge that friends were remembering his family in prayer. Typically he wrote to the Rev. and Mrs. John Bickersteth at Ashburnham Place, Sussex: "I feel greatly encouraged by your deep concern for my family in China. Though I have not heard from them yet I am greatly comforted by 2 Timothy 1:12, 'I am persuaded that he is able to keep that which I have committed unto him against that day'."

If there were no letters from China there was a regular correspondence from former members of the Church now scattered throughout the world. From Hong Kong, a newly-wed wrote: "God's mercies to us, so unworthy of them, are without number. Having obtained my Ph.D. I am now lecturer in English at United College of the Chinese University. Beatrice also completed her music course at the same time and will do some part-time teaching."

A very talented art student who became a Christian during her stay in London wrote to him from Toronto: "I have been here for six weeks now. Time seems to fly since I came to Canada. I have been attending the Chinese Presbyterian Church here and the

Bible studies at the Chinese Gospel Church. I have found it a bit trying, settling down to this new environment, but I am truly grateful for the absolute assurance that this is where God himself has brought me and he will not leave me."

"Nothing," he would say on receiving such letters, "nothing can make me more happy than to know that our scattered members are still going on strong in the Lord."

Members returning to West Malaysia would write telling him of new arrivals in London. "A week ago, a friend requested me to help his friend's son by introducing him to the Chinese Church in London. He will be reaching London on September 14, and will study at the Kilburn Polytechnic. His English is now good. He is a home-loving boy spending most of his time growing orchids and catching butterflies."

Parents worried about their children in London wrote to him. From Kuala Lumpur a father wrote typically: "Dear Rev. Father, I shall be much obliged if you will kindly advise my daughter . . . she is young and the slightest thought may lead her away. I am not a Christian, but I don't go against her in her belief, for I was brought up in a Catholic school." His daughter has played a key role in the Chinese Church. During the riots in Malaya in 1969 her parents home was burned down and they lost their business. They were one of several families for whom it was a privilege for the Christians in London to send practical help.

He remained a father to the Chinese however far they had gone from London. In May 1969 he wrote to Charles and Mary Tang. The letter is significant because it is an example of hundreds individually written.

We have just heard about the riots in Kuala Lumpur between the Malays and the Chinese. We have prayed about this racial clash, especially remembering you all and the other brothers and sisters in that city. May God protect you and use you to witness in such a time as this. [He went on to give them the news from Britain]. In Manchester, Swee Hwa and Esther have done well especially in the Sunday-school work. They have about forty Chinese children . . . The Yorkshire Christian

Fellowship has also been greatly blessed by God. The work in Edinburgh is very encouraging. I spoke on Sunday there to more than forty people mostly restaurant workers ... Last Monday Frank Cheung and I drove to Glasgow: there are more than twenty Chinese restaurants and as far as we know only three Christians among them ... In the evening we went to Greenock where there are a few Chinese students and three restaurants.

In Britain the number of fellowships continued to grow. They were established by teams of young people, led by Stephen, making repeated visits. Weary journeys and tired feet were easily forgotten in his company. In rain and fog and snow, late at night and on hot summer days, in tight new shoes or when the ground was frozen, the small groups would sally forth. He would first investigate the number and location of Chinese in an area, draw up a visitation plan, and then choose young members to accompany him. He went with them on the first two or three visits, then challenged them to go back every fortnight, or even every weekend to establish a new witness.

"They're too inexperienced," some advised him. "They will make mistakes."

"Don't be frightened by their mistakes," he replied. "The young learn by them."

When the weather was very bad a new companion might hesitantly mention it, but only once.

"I cannot sit down beside a fire though I have every right to do so as an old man," he would beam. "And you are young."

To Chinese students and nurses Stephen did seem a very old man. In China he would have retired, but his age was a challenge to them. Those he visited were moved and humbled that he should call on them. They gathered round to engage in stimulating conversation.

In some restaurants he met Chinese waiters who spoke a different dialect, but they were nevertheless honoured by his call. With permission, he would go into the kitchen, stand by the stove, and make friends. The young people watched, falsely believing he had a special technique. When there were setbacks he was content that God was the judge of failure, not man.

There were enthusiasts who suggested grandiose schemes, but these had little appeal for him.

"Christ called men one by one," he pointed out. "By a word, or a look, or just by loving, he changed a life."

His method was to get everyone to do something, however small. "By love, serve one another." Through this means fellowships were formed in Birmingham, Manchester, Leeds, Oxford, Bristol, Bradford, Glasgow, Aberdeen, Edinburgh and St. Albans.

In the last two years of his life he constantly said: "There is so much land to be possessed," thinking of the thousands of Chinese in Europe, "and I cannot do it any more but you *must* do it."

As a teacher he taught by example, but the physical strain was telling. It was seen in unguarded moments and for some while was only evident to those close to him. Mostly, he was master of his spirit, his smile always there, but his vigour was beginning to ebb. The dogged perseverance, however, did not easily slumber.

I I

The Man

THE MOST PRECIOUS TIME in the Chinese Church in London was the monthly communion service, when the bread and wine were shared, and we thought of those in China. The oceans and the continents between us disappeared, the miles that separated temporarily vanished. Sensitive spirits felt so close to our brethren that the door might have opened and Stephen's former students and fellow church members have shyly entered . . .

"Take, eat, this is my body which is broken for you . . ."

Were their hands still outstretched, outstretched to receive, outstretched in prayer?

This was the family gathering, and the family was worldwide, of every nation and tongue. It was the hour when the material world shrivelled, when nothing mattered but to please God.

In mind I would slip back into my father's Presbyterian church, surrounded by trees, on a hillside in northern China, where I had spent my childhood. Now the church which he had built was no longer used for worship. How had they fared, those members who had wanted to spoil his children with small luxuries? Like me, they would have grown older, some would have died. The girls who sat with me would have children of their own, rapidly growing up. Did their parents fear to mention God?

Although there were tight limits on religious practice in China it did continue in some form until 1966. In 1965 there was one Protestant theological college. This was closed in 1966.

In the late summer of that year the Red Guard militants closed every remaining church; searching the homes of members, destroying Bibles, and any religious literature and persecuting believers. Anti-Christian, anti-Buddhist and anti-Muslim Red Guard posters were displayed. The Red Guards were out finally to destroy old ideas, old culture, old customs and old habits.

But secret communion services, using the same words as we did, continued. In storerooms and farm outhouses, in kitchens and beneath the stars, wherever there was privacy, small groups gathered, and at the communion table we were linked with them.

Until 1964 a communion offering was taken in London and sent to Shanghai through an address in Hong Kong. In return came an occasional letter, again via Hong Kong. Then it became impossible.

In the sixties a surviving Christian in Shanghai, using familiar tunes, wrote new hymns. Some of these found their way to London and were sung at our church. Biblical in expression, written in Chinese, they were translated into English, and forged stronger links. We studied them minutely to find clues about the spirit of the Church at home. They emphasised Christ's call to his children to bravely, steadfastly, take up the cross. They told of great opportunities to make a sacrifice for God.

Stephen treasured these slips of paper, allowing no one to touch them, any copies being made painstakingly by himself. He would not let the original out of his sight. It was not great prose or verse, but great faith, and he treated them as the early Church must have regarded a scrap of parchment from the Apostle Paul.

In nearly every hymn there was the hope of the second coming of Christ, a daily expectation with many suffering Christians, and a reminder to those in London also to be ready.

The prayer of Christ, in John's Gospel, seemed apt.

"And now I am no more in the world, but these are in the world, and I come to thee, Holy Father, keep through thine own name those whom thou hast given me, that they may be one, as we are ... I pray not that thou shouldest take them out of the world, but that thou shouldest keep them from evil. They are not of the world, even as I am not of the world."

At the end of the communion service there was a spirit of expectancy. Each saw through a glass darkly, but it was better than not seeing at all.

One day Stephen feared what he saw. In our private Church office he found an unauthorised young man methodically copying out a list of those who worshipped with us. His vague suspicions had been partly confirmed. He had been alert for several weeks.

The young man looked stunned. For a moment there was silence, but Stephen did not want an angry confrontation. He withdrew the list, explaining that it was private, but he remained troubled. Many parents had placed their sons and daughters in his charge while they studied in London, and he did not wish either them or their parents to get involved in a political situation.

"We're guardians. We must be watchful," he told those in the office. "Doors and drawers must be locked. Strangers must be challenged."

Stephen rarely spoke about politics.

"The good news of the Gospel of Jesus Christ," he would say, "is what my country needs, and the Chinese everywhere, and that is my business."

He could never visualise any deep understanding between Christianity and Communism with its rejection of God, but he was positively for Christ, rather than anti-anything

"Is your Church anti-Mao?" he was pressed. The question came most in America.

"What Chairman Mao needs, like me, like you, is a Saviour," he would reply, "and Christ is that Saviour."

The Chinese in the West are secure. They develop their businesses, in South Africa opening supermarkets and in Britain restaurants: buy their homes and bring up their families without fear, being absorbed into the local community and contributing to it. Only rarely are there incidents which disturb.

In London in 1968 there were violent clashes between members of the Chinese Legation and the police. A few policemen were hurt and within hours the Chinese in large cities became targets for abuse from a tiny minority. The Englishman believed in defending his policemen, and a tin of paint was angrily splashed across the door of the Chinese Church centre.

While we were at a Chinese conference in Ashburnham, near the Sussex coast, demands that the Chinese return home were plastered across our doors in London during the night. As we drove back to London I pulled up at a road junction. A man put his head to the open window with an alarming glare.

"We don't want you here," he stormed. "Go home."

There was a couple of seconds before the lights changed and I asked what was wrong.

"You've struck our police," he said with disgust.

I apologised, and explained that the Chinese were not usually like that. I asked him to accept my apology for the untypical incident.

Stephen was an evangelist. "Oh, I long for souls, precious Chinese souls, our people to know him," he would say.

Stephen was a caring pastor. In the opinion of some however, judged homiletically, he was not a distinguished preacher. His sermons lacked cohesion and tended to be long-winded. When he was carried away by the occasion, he was oblivious of time.

He spoke for half an hour at the wedding service of his assistant, Pastor Chua Wee-hian. Later at the reception he spent another twenty-five minutes talking glowingly about Wee-hian and his bride, King Ling. Wee-hian tried to signal him to stop for there were five other speakers. The bride and bridegroom missed the train that was to take them on their honeymoon, but Wee-hian bore him no grudge. Now General Secretary of the International Fellowship of Evangelical students he remembers rather how Stephen was in intimate touch with God. This is what distinguished him, together with his gifts as an evangelist. He had compassion, warmth, friendliness, and a robust concern for people.

Wherever he went he carried a notebook with him which he called 'the book of life'. When he was instrumental in leading someone to Christ, as soon as they had professed faith, he or she was encouraged to write down his or her decision in the book. The entries read, "Today ... I accept Jesus Christ as my Saviour and Lord." He loved to quote these. In the newsletters he would print the names. The editor tried to argue with him.

"Pastor, why must we have the same entry again and again. The readers will get tired of this column of converts."

"No," he replied, "if we don't have this list of names, it shows that God is not at work in our midst. When He works, people come and trust Him."

It was this sense of God's presence and the expectation that God was working, that led Stephen to many wonderful adventures.

His greatness was in his ability to trust his co-workers and to provide opportunities for them to exercise their gifts. He rarely interfered with the young people when they organised their conferences. He rejoiced when they used their talents and gifts for God. He spoke of the Chinese Church as a training ground for spiritual leaders. Many ex-members of the London Church, now scattered throughout the world, witness that it was with him that they were first inspired to serve God.

He was criticised for his constant talk about conversion, and asked for more doctrinal teaching on other topics. He tried to respond, but whatever his text the desire to see men turn to Christ surfaced. The first sermon he preached in the London Church was based on the Apostle Paul's words: "For I have determined to know nothing among you save Christ and him crucified." It was the sermon he went on preaching and living.

He liked his young people to go to Westminster Chapel, London, to hear Dr. Martyn Lloyd-Jones on Sunday mornings, but when they returned bubbling with enthusiasm he warned: "Do not build up your heads, if you have little legs to walk on."

He himself loved the preaching of this celebrated Welshman

who after qualifying as a physician gave up his medical career to become a minister. They had in common that they both switched careers in mid-stream, but while the doctor believed that preaching is the highest and greatest and most glorious calling to which anyone can be called, Stephen was satisfied to be a witness, anywhere.

On several occasions Dr. Lloyd-Jones showed special kindness to him.

Stephen lived in an atmosphere of prayer, but when faced with a problem he did not habitually say, "Let us pray". He went to bed after midnight, but each morning, about 5 a.m. he sat up and prayed and read. This early morning habit was probably inspired by John Wesley whose life he had closely studied. As a Methodist he had heard Wesley's advice to fix some part of every day for private meditation.

"You may acquire the taste which you have not," wrote Wesley. "What is tedious at first, will afterwards be pleasant. Whether you like it or not, read and pray daily. It is for your life; there is no other way; else you will be a trifler all your days, and a pretty superficial preacher. Do justice to your own soul; give it time and means to grow. Do not starve yourself any longer. Take up your cross and be a Christian altogether. Then will all the children of God rejoice (not grieve) over you."

He read the *Forty-Four Sermons* by Wesley and whenever he could escorted his guests to Wesley's Chapel, London. Then he would linger in the place where Susannah Wesley was buried. If there was time they would go to the plaque marking the spot where Wesley's heart was 'strangely warmed'.

Wesley was concerned with caring for his converts and training them to be witnesses. In his *Journal* he wrote after visiting Tanfield, near Newcastle:

From the terrible instances I met with there (and indeed in all parts of England), I am more and more convinced that the devil himself desires nothing more than that the people of any place should be half-awakened and then left to themselves to fall asleep again. Therefore I determine, by the grace of God,

not to strike one blow in any place where I cannot follow the
blow.

The Chinese Christian fellowships catered for Stephen's converts, but he went to great lengths to see they also became part of a
local church. He believed in striking and following the blow.

His sermons included references to Chinese characters. One
of the Chinese characters for sin is composed of two characters,
he would explain. One is 'net' and the other is 'wrong', then he
would tell how men are caught in a net of wrong-doing, from
which they can never escape themselves.

Sermons can reveal a preacher's soul. Stephen's missionary
motivation was constantly projected, as was his personal experience of God. He would tell how he had known the awfulness
of sin, and sought how to deal with it. Then God granted him
a glimpse of a crucified Lord who had already solved this
problem for him. A sinner and a Saviour equalled a child of
God.

But people remembered him rather than his sermons, his
love for Christ and for them rather than his words.

"I remember," one writes, "how the young people loved him
and hung round him. I remember the degree days when he
represented their parents. Especially the one when the Queen
Mother presented the degrees to one young student who
received both medical and surgical degrees in one year. How
proud he was."

He loved [writes another], "to invite all the foreign missionary students to an evening squash in his room, and how they
gathered round him. Happy, most informal gatherings making all new arrivals feel at home; cups of tea, Chinese sweet
'eats', much laughter over language tangles after a day of
hard study. He entered into it all, making each feel so
welcome, and drawing out each to say or sing something.
The singing in various languages, testimonies in broken
English, dispelled all shyness of the newcomers. The pastor's
closing fatherly prayer for them, their dear ones, their

studies, their hopes of service in far lands, and the blessing
of the Lord to be their portion, made a treasured memory.

I was converted at his meeting in Leeds in October, 1969 [a
young graduate writes]. The meeting was just one of those
incidents that slotted into God's design for me. In July I had
graduated in mechanical engineering with first-class honours
and was offered a job at a research establishment near
Cambridge. It was inconceivable to me at this time of
achieving a major objective I should develop a sense of
depression and anticlimax but I did just that. For the first
time I questioned seriously the meaning of life. Then God
started to move. I dropped the job in Cambridge and stayed
in Leeds to do research. During that summer I was in
Sheffield for a vacation job. My landlady was a fine
Christian, and for the first time I was confronted with
Christ. Not long after my return to Leeds I received an
invitation from the Yorkshire Chinese Christian fellowship
inviting me to a welcome party. On Saturday October 18 I
went along to listen to Pastor Wang. His message was
simple, with no glamour, but it burst on to me in all its
reality and freshness. At the end of the meeting I felt
overpowered by God's spirit. I knew I had to choose then,
and I chose God's way.

Each morning he planned out his day in a small book, writing
in either Chinese or English, listing his duties numerically. He
would tick them off one by one. In his first years in Britain he had
been unable to type and had written hundreds of letters by hand.
Later he became a two-finger typist, then had the luxury of a
shorthand-typist, but he was not good at dictation for he kept
getting carried away. Letters became like sermons.

He was generous with his money as well as his words, distribut-
ing it freely, but he enjoyed giving presents, most of all if the gift
was for a baby newly-born to a couple whose wedding service he
had conducted. It was impossible to restrain him, but although he
spent little on himself he dressed with care. If there was a crease

on the collar of his shirt, he would not wear it, although the cuffs might be frayed. I challenged him when I saw him looking in the mirror, checking his appearance, as I thought.

"Mary, there have been days when I have been alone and had nobody to talk to but that friend in the mirror," he said. "My friend in the mirror never gets angry, is always sympathetic. I laugh, he laughs. I cry, he cries."

We hated packing for him. His wife had excelled in this, but he regularly complained on his return that we had not packed enough socks, handkerchiefs, or that we had left out the shoe polish. His wife would have known exactly what he needed. In the corner of the suitcase, he explained, she would hide money for the children and the servants of the Chinese homes he visited. Her judgment was impeccable. When he returned home he had nothing left, but he was never short. Thinking how we had miscalculated we bowed in shame.

Stephen, like many men, lost or misplaced his possessions. The lady superintendent of the House of Rest, where he made his home for many years, made extensive notes on Sunday mornings as she listened to Dr. Lloyd-Jones. Her father had been a C.I.M. missionary, she had been born in China, and she cared affectionately for Stephen. The affection was tested however when she loaned him her priceless collection of sermon notes made at Westminster Chapel and he lost them.

When he misplaced his books he had usually given them away. He brought few books with him from China, but from his student days he had a love of books and found it difficult to resist making a purchase even if it meant parting with a last pound-note. He passed them on to students and others in the Church.

He was an optimist, sometimes, some thought, too optimistic. He could commit his colleagues to a course of action without consultation, but they learned that he was more far-sighted, or had greater faith. A colleague in China described him as not easy to work with, a man who went his own way in opposition to school committees, who resented the disciplines imposed by others. Of those years it was true. There were upheavals when he was a thorn in the flesh of Methodist missionaries, for the spiritual crisis which changed the direction of his life did not take place until he was fifty and resident in England. When questioned with regard to those earlier years of accomplishment, he would say, "Past — obscure".

Phyllis Thompson, a missionary in China from 1936 to 1951, recalls his dignity and poise.

> He was tall and broad-shouldered for a Chinese, and his presence was impressive. Those of us who knew realised how very lonely he was, but his hospitality at the Chinese Church centre made the place what it was. When he was there, it seemed to be a home, where all could be sure of a welcome.
>
> I was impressed by his preaching — its clarity and its Christ-centredness. This was very marked. He was a *Chinese* pastor and he liked the services in London to be in Chinese, but he graciously made concessions to the English-speaking people present. In fact, he was a Chinese through and through, although he wore a Western suit. It was remarkable that he should arrive in Britain, an unknown refugee, and without any powerful backing, have established the Chinese Church in London and influenced so many young Chinese, students especially.

Some may have thought his love of food was wholesome, others a failing. Visiting so many Chinese restaurants had compensations, yet he often neglected his meals, paying little attention to the hour if busily occupied. Those who were with him never knew if there would be a lunchtime break or not. Young people in the Church, concerned for his well-being, prepared meals; once grace had been said he relished every portion.

Graces could become long extemporary prayers, but his public prayers in church were written in advance, probably because he prayed first in Chinese and then repeated the sentences in English. He gave the same attention to preparing the prayer as to his sermon, believing that leading the church in talking to God was as important as talking to the church about God.

He was not a man of prayer in the sense of a David Brainerd, but at the close of the day he would pray for half an hour or longer. His mind was constantly on his people. When he prayed it was for his people, mentioning their names. These were written in the book before him.

Although being parted from his family was a great burden, a grief which his friends knew about, in conversation he usually brushed the topic aside. Mr. Harding, talking to him one day about his family, could not avoid being aware of the grief in his eyes. His usual question was: "Any news from the Far East?" The usual reply, a shake of the head. On this particular day Mr. Harding tried to get out a few words of sympathy and concern. The reply was characteristic: "When I am down, I look up to God, and when I look up, I am always blessed." Fred Harding recalled the words of the English writer, Izaak Walton:

> Of this blest man, let him just praise be given,
> Heaven was in him before he was in heaven.

Nothing, absolutely nothing — the lack of news from China, the absence of his family, the hardship of being a lonely exile — could hold his eyes down. He paraphrased the words of St. Paul in Romans 10, 1: "My heart's desire and prayer to God for China is, that they might be saved."

He had a quiet dignity, gracious manner and showed respectful attention to what people said. His enthusiasm was infectious. New acquaintances were impressed by his breadth of knowledge, his command of English, and by his great devotion. He endeared himself by so many loving gestures, such as the gracious way with which he got up from his desk and walked forward, with hand outstretched, to greet a visitor.

12

Goodbye Pastor

MY PARENTS, my brother Martin and his family, and I lived together in the inner suburbs of London. We all wanted to give Stephen a home and so he came to us and became another grandpa to Martin's children. Martin, always clever with his hands, found ways of using to the best advantage the limited space we shared, including making a beautiful table which at the end of a meal became a decorative wallpiece. There were days when we thought we would have to build upwards to find the space we needed, but our lives were enriched by his presence.

My father, although retired from the ministry, had spent one year after his arrival in Europe as pastor of the Church in Paris, but in 1970 we were all united again. That year Stephen had two major operations. I was in America when he had the first. Cables were sent instructing me to return. I arrived at a London hospital after midnight. He was critically ill but asleep when a nurse took me to his bedside.

"Mary, you're back," he said, when he opened his eyes. "When did you come?"

"He is happier now," the night superintendent told me. "You should go home and return in the morning."

After that I was allowed to stay with him whenever I wished. A few weeks later on May 2 a second operation was necessary.

"Mary, I am weaker and weaker. I do not think there is any hope but I have peace in my heart," he said five days afterwards.

On May 17 we believed that God had touched his body for he began to get better. He was to be spared to us until the following year, using the precious months to share his vision regarding the work he had founded.

In February 1971 he became ill and reported a swelling on his stomach. He felt faint in the bathroom and called me. I put him to bed, afraid. I kept a diary, in which as always I called him uncle.

Saturday February 20

I took uncle to see Dr. Lee. After his examination Dr. Lee asked him to dress and took me next door. He wrote two words 'liver secondaries' on a piece of paper which he handed to me. This confirmed my fear. I felt I could not accept, but I returned to help him dress. I was shaking inwardly, but had to appear calm.

Sunday February 21

Went to church in afternoon. Rev. Hill preached for him. Afterwards I asked a nursing sister at University College Hospital to make an appointment for us.

Tuesday February 23

Arrived at the hospital at 2.30, but he was so weak that I had to put him in a wheel-chair. The professor's assistant examined him, and suggested he remained in hospital. I courteously refused because I had promised uncle earlier that I would not leave him in hospital. After x-ray and blood examination I was called by the doctor. He told me the diagnosis was liver secondaries and that he might have two or three months to live. My heart was torn. I had to pray before I came back to him. I told God I don't understand. I said to uncle he must rest and have extra nutrition. On the return journey I had to be very careful in driving because of the state of my mind.

Wednesday February 24

Uncle is very weak with great pain. Went to the centre for a short while. I cannot continue to work in the office or to speak publicly because this is the time he needs me most. I do not want to regret afterwards. Telephoned Pastor Hsuan that tomorrow night I will visit him around 10 p.m.

Thursday February 25

It looks as if I need to go to our Leeds fellowship this weekend. (Uncle had been booked). When I talked with him about my speaking engagement tonight at St. Albans he said I should go. On my way I dropped in at the centre — everything was all right. As I drove to St. Albans my heart was not with me. I was very empty and lonely. Maybe because I am so accustomed to him sitting beside me. I got to Fred Harding's home about 7 p.m. I couldn't eat supper and I told him and Margaret what had happened. Fred went to speak for me and after prayer I went to Pastor Hsuan's home. I was grateful to him and Sue for their kindness and sympathy, but suddenly I felt the heavy responsibility on me. Arrived home at 11 p.m. and he was resting.

Friday February 26

Father helped me to move the couch to his room so I can look after him in the night.

Saturday February 27

I left home at 8.30 for King's Cross. Dr. Lilian Pang came to our home to take care of him. I visited Bradford and St. Luke's hospital, also Huddersfield hospital in the evening, where more than forty nurses came to the meeting. Four nurses accepted Christ. It snowed heavily on our way back to Leeds.

Sunday February 28

I spent the morning in quiet to prepare for the afternoon. My heart is in London. Many people came to the service and by request I spoke on stewardship then hurriedly I caught the train for London. I became impatient because the train was rather slow.

Wednesday March 3

To see the one I love suffering like this makes my heart very

painful. I hold him and cry. I can't help it. He said, "Don't cry for
it grieves me. Be strong in the Lord. Will you continue my work or
do you have any other plans?" I was hurt because he suggested
other plans. I told him, "You know." He said, "I know but I want
you to tell me again." I promised that with God enabling I would
do my utmost to continue his work.

Thursday March 4

I phoned Dr. Lee who was most kind. As he was not in the
district I asked if I should get another doctor. "I'll come wherever
he is," he said. He is worse every day and the swelling in the liver is
bigger. I talked with Lilian about the possibility of chemotherapy
and decided to contact the hospital and ask the professor's opinion,
but I fear the side effect of this treatment will give him much more
pain.

Friday March 5

He asked me to read the fourth and fifth chapters of Second
Corinthians. We talked about the test of our faith. Do we truly
believe in the resurrection, that while our outer nature is wasting
away our inner nature is being renewed every day? Yes, if the
earthly tent we live in is destroyed we have a building from God
eternal in the heavens. What is mortal may be swallowed up by life.
We both believe but suddenly my emotion is bigger than my
reason. In the evening Moo Him came so I could go to the Church
committee. I shared with them what we learned this morning.
Again I felt the heaviness of the burden. Moo Him decided to stay
for the night to look after him: he is so kind. Frank came from
Birmingham. I called him to my room and told him about pastor's
condition. He cried, his love for him is very deep.

Saturday March 6

Contacted our Churches and fellowships asking for united
prayer after worship tomorrow.

Sunday March 7

At 3 a.m. he asked me to write the following words: "From 12 to

3 a.m. I am very mixed up in my dream. I found myself in a castle park which was occupied by one king and his two servants. No one was allowed to march in. All those who tried were defeated. The government wanted to take over this place but permission was refused. Because of the continued fighting the two servants surrendered but the old king still went on fighting alone refusing to surrender. And suddenly I woke up. God has a lesson for me which I feel rather important in my present illness." I did not go to church. Pastor Hsuan preached. 7 p.m. some young people came. They sang and prayed for him. He cried with tears and I held his hands.

Monday March 8

Professor says we should not try chemotherapy. Uncle told me today that one famous doctor at home in China before he died was determined to have a walk every day. When he was too weak to do this he went out in a rickshaw. He asked me to put my ear against his lips. He said very weakly. "I am grateful to you for your love. You know I always treasured this." I smiled and said, "You never told me before." We both laughed, then I told him if God was going to take him I would not know how to face life. He looked at me with a rebuke and said God's strength and grace is sufficient for you.

Tuesday March 9

He told me that all his books were mine. I have always told you, he said, to spend more time reading the Bible and other books. This room should be your study. The best way you can remember me is to study to be prepared more for the work God has for you.

Wednesday March 10

He sat up in the chair for an hour in the morning and afternoon. "I would like you to draw some money from my bank," he said, "for your parents. This is a very little way I can show my gratitude to them for allowing their daughter to look after me like this." He saw my tears and said, "Don't be so sad.

Before God and man you have done your best for me." I said that
when the opportunity came I would send money to China for him.

Thursday March 11

With a great struggle he got up this morning. Dr. Lee came at 3
p.m. I gave him the pot of azaleas which uncle had asked me to
buy for the doctor's wife. The doctor told me he might have two
or three weeks to live. He asked the doctor to let nature take its
course and the doctor explained there was nothing he could do.
At the door the doctor told me how he admired his devotion and
courage. I thanked him for his kindness and he replied that
nobody could help but love and respect him. He prescribed
Valium which helped him in his sleep.

Friday March 12

Because he was so drowsy I only gave him half Valium. In the
afternoon he said he wanted me to be recognised legally as his
daughter. "Will you ask your parent's permission?" he asked. I
said they would not object. "It's too late to contact our solicitor
but first thing on Monday morning you must ask him to come to
see me." Pearl came to keep him company in the night so I went
to bed at 1 a.m. She called me at 4 a.m. and said that he needed
me. He didn't want me to leave the room.

Saturday March 13

He had a little broth this morning. I am heart-broken because
of his suffering yet amazed at my courage which comes from God.
He said he was more comfortable after I massaged his right side
gently. Moong Seng arrived from Bristol in the afternoon to help
me. His pulse is weak and irregular. His breathing is not even. I
have an unspeakable fear about life without him. Although everyone insists I rest I fear to leave the room because I don't know
how long I may still have him. Chee Ming came with the family
and was very upset.

Sunday March 14

There was a strange calm in the room this morning. Everything

absolutely still. His heart beat is weak and pulse irregular. I feel
so sad but holding his hand I felt the sweetness and the wonderful
presence of God. I thanked God throughout the whole day for the
years I have been given and for what I have learned from him. No
other person has influenced me more. I thanked God for his
fatherly love and care. Suddenly all the things he gave to me
became precious but life is much more precious. I felt a knife
cutting my heart when I see his tired face express pain. I can only
place him in the hands of our God. He wanted me to go to church,
Kwei Lan will come to nurse him, but I decided not to go. I told
Hoe Weng, "God might call him home in a couple of days
therefore we should not restrain the young people from coming to
see him tonight." Fred Harding and Margaret arrived at 4 p.m. I
talked with them about funeral arrangements. At 5 p.m. Kwei Lan
called me and I found he was breathing with great difficulty. Seven
or eight times I breathed mouth to mouth into him. He could not
speak, but I talked to him. We had previously arranged that he
would nod if he agreed and just shake his head if not. Before I
asked Fred to pray I asked him whether he had peace of heart. He
nodded with a smile. I asked if he wanted to thank Fred for his
friendship in the last twenty years. He nodded immediately. I
believe he could see but he was so helpless like a child. In the
evening many car loads of young people arrived quietly and two by
two came to the room and stood silently beside him. Every one was
tearful. Many said quietly "Goodbye Pastor" before they walked
out. Chor Hin gathered them in the living room to pray. I joined
them for a while and I believe in life nothing can touch me more
than this experience. Their love towards their shepherd-father-
counsellor-friend was too obvious. Finally Peter and Ernest arrived
and stayed until midnight. Frank phoned and I asked him to drive
to London immediately. He arrived at 2 a.m. Together with May
Lee and Kwei Lan we were around his bed for the whole night,
except I slept for a little on the sofa.

Monday March 15

At 9 a.m. I relieved May Lee who was with him. He was very
calm and serene. There was no sign of pain or struggling and I was

with him alone. From time to time he would lift up his hands towards Heaven. I shall forever treasure this half hour in which I recalled the grace of God and his faithfulness with thanksgiving for the way he has helped me in the love of Christ. To me he was a pioneer. At 9.30 I called everyone to come in — Frank, May Lee, Kwei Lan, Kah Thuan. I knelt before him and led in prayer in Chinese holding his hands which were already cold. I thanked God for his life, for the good fight he had fought, for the race he had run, for the faith he had kept and asked God to challenge us anew as we continued his work that a double portion of his spirit would be upon us. At 9.37 a.m. he lifted up his hands and God took him to himself. Looking into his face I saw God. I kissed him three times.

Shortly before Stephen died my four-year-old nephew, David, came in to say goodbye as was his custom before leaving for school.

"Goodbye, Pastor Grandpa, I'm going, and I'll be good."

His little hand touched Pastor Grandpa's for the last time.

Pastor John Hsuan conducted the funeral service in the Talbot Tabernacle, where the Chinese Church had been meeting for its Sunday services. Dr. McIntosh was present from America, and colleagues from Holland and France. Mr. Harding who had been the treasurer for twenty-one years spoke of his love and friendship.

To know him was to love him and to want to serve him and to support him through thick and thin. He had his private grief. Most of you know he was a political exile from his own country and that his dear ones in China were cut off from any fellowship with him. One day I saw his face suffused with grief. I told him I was so sorry I could not enter into this sorrow. He said "When this grief comes upon me I look up into the face of Christ."

Before Stephen was taken ill, we had attended a funeral at the Putney Vale cemetery. As I drove him through the gates, he said, "Mary, this is a beautiful place!" Since we laid his body there I have returned in the early morning to listen and to pray. He is not there, but I love the quiet and calm.

A memorial service was held in Westminster Chapel, London. Among the large number of Chinese were distinguished men and women, but most of all Stephen would have been pleased to see some of his Methodist friends. They may have thought of him again as the headmaster of Tangshan school, a position which he held for so long that he imagined he would remain in it until retirement, but in academically losing his life he had found it and grown to greater stature. In Charles Wesley's words:

> To spend, and to be spent, for them
> Who have not yet my Saviour known.

13

The China Letter

WAS STEPHEN'S WIFE ALIVE? If so, how could she be told of his death? There had been no news from her since 1965. Letters had remained unanswered and a businessman who visited Peking from the West found no trace of her.

Stephen died believing that she and Sung Ling had been dead for several years. But his tender love for her had not died, and because there remained a tiny hope, he had prayed for her daily. Before 1965 she had uncertain health and high blood pressure. There were political reasons why the letters may have stopped, not least the Cultural Revolution in 1966, but as year succeeded year despair set in.

"What do you think?" he would ask. "I feel as if she is alive, I imagine I hear her voice, but I'm growing tired of being disappointed."

At the beginning we reassured him, looking through the post for her handwriting, but expectation gradually became a grey morning agony.

"Anything from China?"

We shook our heads.

Eric Gordon, an English journalist, was an eye-witness of the Cultural Revolution in Peking and saw thousands of Red Guards changing the face of the city almost overnight. The Imperial Palace was renamed the Palace of Blood and Tears. The Pei Hei Park was called the Workers, Peasants and Soldiers Park. His hotel was renamed the Revolutionary Guest House. Antique furniture, jewellery, and fashionable clothes were taken from private homes. Professors, former landlords and sometimes old women were made to clear the streets as a punishment for past misdeeds, and there were rumours of many suicides.

In such a city anything could have happened to anyone.

Mr. Gordon wrote in his book *Freedom is a Word*:

Yet despite the upheavals of the Cultural Revolution, the confusion, the rumours, the interminable meetings, my colleagues still found it possible to separate their private lives from the wildly hectic political atmosphere of the revolution during the day. Nothing was so astounding, as to how they persisted in living ordinary family lives in the evenings and Sundays. Sunday, in particular, was still a day to be set aside for family life with shopping expeditions to town, walks in the park, outings to the western hills or to the zoo.

He tells of one of the keenest Red Flag members, a young girl, who could drown her opponents in a non-stop barrage of words, but who on Sundays became magically transformed, devoting her day to her newborn baby, of whom she was intensely proud. Between arguments and meetings she would proudly bring out a photograph taken at the zoo. "Doesn't he look lovely?" A moment later she was hurrying to an emergency Red Flag meeting.

In his dreams Stephen had visualised his wife with her grandchildren, taking them shopping in the Peking streets, and to see the inner city, once the Forbidden City, now a museum. Peking had extended considerably since he left. With a population of 7,300,000 in 1958 it was among the biggest cities in China. To the north and west of the city there had been residential development, with the industrial belt extending to the east including cotton mills, and iron and steel works.

He had lovingly preserved the earlier letters, since 1948, in which his wife had written freely, urging him to serve God, and not to neglect Bible reading or prayer. She sought information about Cambridge, and the Chinese Church, wanting to share in all his enterprises.

Later, the content was more reserved, and the nature of the correspondence changed. He kept with the letters a framed picture of the family taken before he travelled to England. In the early sixties he received a new family photograph. Only Sung Ling and himself were missing. He superimposed one of himself, placing it by his wife, but doing it almost choked him.

Before 1965 he was able to send money to his wife through the Bank of China, and parcels listing on the outside details of the contents. His doctor son needed a watch. He wished to send the best in Europe, but a girl in the Church had an old and trusted one, completely reliable. When it was received in China a £50 tax had to be paid. He transferred the sum. Because of this tax, parcels usually contained slightly worn clothes, but in wild moments he dreamed of a shopping spree, buying all the luxuries which would gladden the heart of a woman, and demonstrate his affection.

"Do not write," her last letter had urged.

For months he restrained himself. When he did write there was no response.

He heard of a businessman who had official business in Peking. He contacted him and asked if on his next visit he would look up his wife. He told him where she lived and gave the address. Stephen had not seen the house for it was purchased after his departure, in a dilapidated condition, and he had contributed to its repair.

Businessmen are received in China with courtesy and hospitality, often being given V.I.P. treatment. Cars are placed at their disposal and interpreters are made available to accompany them. They are given literature outlining China's achievements. There is a China Council for the Development of International Trade which arranges for them to be met at airports and seen off again.

"If the opportunity occurs I'll do my best," the businessman promised. "But my inquiries may be misinterpreted so I might land in a cell!"

They shook hands.

The days dragged as Stephen waited for his return.

The businessman completed his business in Peking, then went to find Mrs. Wang. To his dismay there was no such street. In the Cultural Revolution the name had been changed.

When Stephen received the news he thanked the businessman and asked about life in the city. It was full of visitors, Asians, Latin Americans, and Africans, for whom Peking was the new Mecca. The old was there, but more evident was the new.

"Peking was an ancient city when New York was a forest and London a small cluster of houses," Stephen boasted.

"And some would say Peking is a finer city today than either," the businessman told him.

A year before his death Stephen finally reached the conclusion that his wife had died. When he became very ill, her name would come to his lips.

"I am getting weaker, but it will be a great comfort for me to see my wife and daughter in Heaven."

In our family prayers at home he would pray for those in China, but sometimes, suddenly he would stop and words would fail him.

"Uncle, if you loved God enough, and your wife and Sung Ling enough, you would not want to delay going to them," I said when he was very ill.

"There's another side to that," he replied. "Because I love God I want to do more down here, but to be reunited will be wonderful."

Nine months after his death, on December 11, 1971, a letter came from China.

It was a Saturday morning and I flicked through the post at the Chinese centre before opening any. There was an airletter from China addressed to Stephen Wang. There was no name on the back of it, but I knew the handwriting. The postmark was December 5. It was sealed and did not seem to have been tampered with.

It had been agreed that I should open all letters for Stephen, but I was afraid to read this. Young people were coming in and out of the office, and normally I would have greeted them, but now I did not turn my head. Summoning my courage I opened it and read the neat Chinese handwriting, in pencil, written a week earlier *by his wife*.

She and the family were well (there was no mention of Sung Ling).*

She wished to remind Stephen that although he was overseas he must continue to serve the Chinese people. Was it possible for him to go to the Chinese Legation to obtain a certificate proving that he loved China, was loyal to his country, and had no anti-revolutionary activities? If he had been alive, and the Legation would have taken his word, he would have given all three assurances. She wrote that they needed furniture, and apparently it was possible again to send remittances from the West.

I placed the letter in my handbag and turned to the other correspondence but it remained before my eyes. I did not know what to do. I remained in the centre until 10.30 p.m. and went home without having mentioned it to anyone. My parents were in bed, but awake, so I told them Stephen's wife was alive and well.

After the Sunday service at the Chinese Church I showed the letter to a friend. We decided that in the name of the Church I should write telling of his death, but a short delay might prepare her for bad news. Further, it gave opportunity for consultation with someone who had known all the family in China. He advised that we should send photographs of the funeral.

I would liked to have gone to China to break the news of Stephen's death, but a letter had to suffice. In it I told how for many years he had been a guide, father, and teacher to Chinese young people, and how his life had been an example to all who knew him. He had served his people by encouraging them to go forward, to act rightly, and by himself being innocent of doing anything which was harmful to China.

I posted it with prayer.

    * In Autumn 1972 word came from China giving hope that Sung Ling was alive.

14

The Vision

WHEN STEPHEN DIED, Pastor John Hsuan, who had been our assistant pastor, in addition to his business responsibilities, became the pastor of the Chinese Church in London, and I was appointed director of the C.O.C.M. It was ten years since I came to England, and was entertained that first weekend in the home of the principal of Oak Hill theological college, the Rev. Maurice Wood, now Bishop of Norwich.

When I arrived for my training at the King Edward Memorial Hospital in West Ealing the matron saw I was apprehensive.

"Don't be frightened, Mary," she said, gently. "You'll be well looked after."

Now with this new responsibility in the C.O.C.M. I needed someone to say the same to me again. Jesus did. In Matthew's Gospel, chapter 14, the disciples were in a boat many furlongs distant from the land, beaten by the waves, the wind against them. And in the fourth watch of the night he came to them, walking on the sea. And they cried out for fear. But immediately he spoke to them — "Take heart, it is I; have no fear."

"Don't be frightened, Mary," Jesus said. "Take heart, it is I; have no fear."

At a service in Norway a lady told me: "Mary, I have been praying for China for forty-six years."

I believe those prayers included me.

Because there is a constitutional guarantee of religious freedom in China, as the country relaxes limited religious worship may be allowed again. Mao himself said that religion cannot be abolished by administrative decree, nor can people be forced not to believe. At first he thought that religion could be obliterated by discussion, criticism, persuasion and education, and not by coercion or repression. When discussion and persuasion failed he introduced tougher methods.

In 1971 *Eternity* published an article *The Incredible Story of China's Growing Church*, by an anonymous veteran observer of the mainland. It suggested that the Church in China is growing in unprecedented numbers, that two years previously a friend of the writer went to Peking and found a church building with some two hundred people worshipping there. In Shanghai there had developed from one church some forty house churches. The writer estimated that one in four hundred people in China had made some kind of profession of faith, in other words that the number of Christians in China had approximately doubled since Communism came into power.

Some experienced mission authorities thought the article questionable, but there is less doubt about its final paragraph.

"God is working in China today in a first century context. It is virtually a modern counterpart to the Acts of the Apostles — God at work in a highly improbable situation, adding to the Church daily such as should be saved."

One cannot generalise about a nation which covers 3,657,765 square miles. For centuries China was in virtual isolation because of the great mountain ranges on the west, and mountain and desert on the north and north-west, and the Pacific ocean to its east.

One cannot generalise about a population of 800 million which by 1990 will be well over 1,000 million, one third of the world's population. There was birth-control in China and support for it lasted one year, then increased production led to official blessing for more babies. By flood control, improved farming techniques, and irrigation, food production has increased to feed the extra mouths.

A contemporary English writer has confessed that reactions to

China tell one far more about the persons who express them than about China. Raymond Dawson in *The Chinese Chameleon* reminds us that much that appears in the western press depends ultimately on translations from the mainland Chinese papers produced by Americans in Hong Kong. "Many comments on modern China are completely lacking in historical sense. They are made against the yardstick of common European practice, not of Chinese history."

In early 1972 ten British doctors visited China. It had taken them two years to arrange the trip, and they were the first British party to visit China for fifteen years. During their stay they saw twelve hospitals in Shanghai, Canton, Nanking, Wasih and Peking. They visited schools and factories, a commune and several villages with the rural medical services. One of the doctors on his return wrote telling me how he had attended a church service in Peking on Palm Sunday. There were no hymnbooks but he sent the written order of service in the new Chinese script. The congregation included elderly Chinese and visitors. He posed several questions through an interpreter but not all were answered.

The service included the Apostles' Creed, a prayer of repentance, and a responsive reading from Isaiah chapter 55: "Seek ye the Lord while he may be found, call upon him while he is near ... For as the heavens are higher than the earth, so are my ways higher than your ways and my thoughts than your thoughts." Holy communion was followed by the hymn, 'Lord dismiss us with thy blessing'.

Was anyone free to attend? The doctor did not know, but we thank God that in Red China, after what appears to have been an almost total ban on Church services since 1966, that there is evidence of some relaxation.

Is the Church ready with Bibles and other literature? Are the Bible societies prepared? The books that will be wanted are not those we read in the West, but new writing by Chinese Christians who understand the culture. It is a burden shared by each of the Chinese fellowships, including the newly formed fellowship in Australia under John Lu.

Stephen's vision included the Chinese everywhere.

"In Europe every Chinese person must be reached with the Gospel," he said. "Our aim should be to witness to each one. But many of you who know Christ must not remain in Europe or America. You've got to go home."

The biggest change that he saw during his last three years was a willingness among young Chinese in the West, when they had completed their training, to return to Asia. Spiritual awakening was turning their eyes eastwards.

He dreamed of a residential centre where they would spend six months before leaving. In the mornings they would study, attending lectures or reading. Study was a prerequisite of evangelism. In Paul's words to young Timothy: "Study to shew thyself approved unto God, a workman that needeth not to be ashamed, rightly dividing the word of truth." In the afternoons and at weekends, they would be knocking on doors and visiting restaurants.

He envisaged about twelve residents, including nurses, with a retired Bible college tutor giving his services. Because the training would be measured in months not years, there would be a constant inflow, to plug the wastage of ability, and to bring that ability, those talents, under God's control.

To purchase such a centre and to provide scholarships is the aim of the Stephen Wang Memorial Fund.

"We must give them such a vision while they are here," he would say, "that they will return to south-east Asia as evangelists in their own professions and be in a state of readiness to enter China if the opportunity comes. They need to be trained to share their faith.

"We are grateful for the magnificent support of C.O.C.M. staff by our brethren in America; for a mini-bus, a car and office equipment; and for gifts from European friends, but when we think of evangelism it is the Chinese who must evangelise their own people."

"It is you," he told the young people, "whom God is calling. To go back to Asia is the first step to China. You must be in government offices, in hospital wards, in schools, in the professions, in every area of influence."

History shows that persecution has often been followed by

revival, when the Spirit of Christ has moved through a Church chastened and purified. After the Boxer uprising 'China for Christ in this generation' became the motto.

"There is every reason to expect a great extension of missionary work in every direction throughout the eighteen provinces of China," mission supporters at home were told in 1904. Every hope was not fulfilled, but consider the statistics.

When Robert Morrison died in 1834 his colleague, William Milne, estimated that it would take one hundred years to gain one thousand Chinese Protestant communicants. A century to get a thousand converts. By 1900 there were 95,946 Church members, and in the next five years this increased to 178,251. In 1922 there were 700,000 and by 1937 960,000. the estimated figure for 1950 was 1,000,000.

"Our God," said Stephen, "is not a foreign god. He is not a Methodist god, or a Presbyterian god. He is our God, the Father of our Lord Jesus Christ. He belongs to the Chinese people. There can be no return to the old days. A foreign-shaped Christianity is not for China."

Twenty-five years is a short period in the history of an ancient nation, but he hoped a lot of lessons had been learned in those years.

When the American writer, Edgar Snow, visited China in 1960 a Roman Catholic priest told him: "For the first time in history we Catholics are in charge of our own Church in China. Always before we were under foreign bishops and domination from abroad." The break between Rome and the Chinese Catholic Church came in 1958.

Having 'cleansed the Church of imperialism' and produced a purely Chinese Church, the Red Armies closed its doors and banned all services. Now, as we have seen, there is evidence that some of the door bolts may be partially withdrawn. The Christ who steps through the door should be in Chinese dress, his piercing, loving words right for Chinese ears.

Stephen was born in the year of the Boxer uprising. It was costly to be a Christian in China then and it has never ceased to be. When he received word in 1950 not to go back to Peking he agonised in spirit and pleaded that God would let him return and rejoin his family. He laboured in prayer for hours, then the words of Jesus came to him: "He who loves father or mother more than me is not worthy of me; and he who does not take up his cross and follow me is not worthy of me. He who finds his life will lose it, and he who loses his life for my sake will find it."

"But Lord," Stephen said, as the need of the Chinese in Europe weighed on him, "I am not a pastor, or a preacher. I'm a teacher who has never been ordained. And who will support me?"

He found himself on his face before God.

"He who receives you," Jesus said, "and he who receives me receives him who sent me. He who receives a prophet because he is a prophet shall receive a prophet's reward, and he who receives a righteous man shall receive a righteous man's reward."

Stephen marvelled that God should have chosen him, for he had a deep humility.

When John Wesley came to die [wrote Dr. Skevington Wood], he had little to bequeath in the way of property. The profits from the sale of his books were to go into the funds of Methodism. A few personal belongings were distributed amongst his friends. He really had nothing to leave except his books, his clothes, his chaise and his loose cash. His true legacy lay in the realm of the Spirit. He left behind a host of converts, to carry on his mission to the nation and the world. This was something no will could list. It represented Wesley's most substantial bequest.

Of a Methodist headmaster, who became an evangelist to the Chinese, the same could be said. Stephen Wang left behind converts scattered over the face of the earth, and to each he had imparted a mission and a vision.

Bibliography

Boyle, Samuel E. (ed.), *Leans to One Side*, Hong Kong, 1950

Burgess, Alan, *The Small Woman*, Evans, 1959

China Handbook, 1970–1, China Publishing Co., Taiwan

Dawson, Raymond, *China Can Take It*, Oxford University Press, 1967

Eternity magazine

Findlay and Holdsworth, *The Wesleyan Methodist Missionary Society*, Epworth Press

Fleming, Peter, *The Siege of Peking*, Rupert Hart-Davis, 1959

Forsyth, Robert (ed.), *The China Martyrs of 1900*, Religious Tract Society, 1904

Fowles, E. R., *Handwritten Manuscripts*, Baptist missionary: China

Glover, Archibald E., *A Thousand Miles of Miracle in China*, Pickering and Inglis

Gordon, Eric, *Freedom is a Word*, Hodder and Stoughton, 1971

Jones, Francis Price, *The Church in Communist China*, Friendship Press

MacInnis, Donald (ed.), *Religious Policy and Practice in Communist China*

Methodist Recorder, 1949–51

Mitchison, Lois, *China*, Thames and Hudson, 1966

Rees, Ronald, *China Can Take It*, Edinburgh House Press

Scott, George A., *China Inland Mission Reports* for 1950, 1951 and 1952; and *In Whose Hand?*

Sewell, William G., *I Stayed in China*, Allen and Unwin, 1966

Stuart, Leighton, *Fifty Years in China*, Random House

Suyin, Han, *A Many Splendoured Thing*, Jonathan Cape, 1952; and *China in the Year 2001*, Watts

Taylor, Mrs. Howard, *Guinness of Honan*, China Inland Mission

Thompson, Phyllis, *A London Sparrow*, Word

Wesley, John, *The Journal*, Epworth

Williamson, H. R., *British Baptists in China, 1845–1952*, Carey-Kingsgate Press; and *The Past Fifty Years in China*, Carey Press

Wood, A. Skevington, *The Burning Heart*, Paternoster Press, 1967

Yutang, Lin, *My Country and My People*, Heinemann